THE
MEMOIRS OF
JEAN LAFFITE

THE
MEMOIRS OF
JEAN LAFFITE

from
Le Journal de Jean Laffite

translated by

Gene Marshall

DEDICATED TO THE MEMORY OF PRICE DANIEL,
FORMER GOVERNOR OF TEXAS,
WHO LOVED THE HISTORY OF JEAN LAFFITE.

To order additional copies of this book, contact:
Xlibris Corporation
1-888-7-XLIBRIS
www.Xlibris.com
Orders@Xlibris.com

CONTENTS

INTRODUCTION

by Robert L. Schaadt

The Journal of Jean Laffite: Its History and Controversy

Provenance is one of the guiding lights of the archival profession whether defined in the context of original order or as the history of ownership. It is a key that leads one to expect to find truth contained in the archives. Archival material is rarely questioned and authorship is seldom a topic of intense discussion. It is assumed that the signer of the letter penned it except when secretaries were known to be employed. Photographs are often dubiously identified by pencil or ink scratches on the back probably made by a grandmother or the third generation before memories fade, but the archivist and the patron rarely question the photograph's identification. Perhaps as a profession we are too trusting and even excessively rely on excellent provenance as a guiding light. Perhaps the patron overly trusts the primary sources and should question them more often.

What does the archivist do when a document is questioned and the provenance is arguable? What is the obligation of an institution when the document not only is challenged, but when it changes history? I have only encountered this situation once in twenty-four years in the profession. As the director of a public history facility since 1983, I have viewed obvious facsimiles, clever forgeries, documents that were claimed to be one thing and were something entirely different resulting in a total loss of market value, and even a few homemade fakes, but the Jean Laffite *Journal* is the only document that falls into that category of true controversy for it changes history. If the Jean Laffite Collection[1] were the John Smith Papers of Liberty County, no one would have questioned them and this article would not be of great interest. The following is the story of the *Journal* of Jean Laffite and its controversy from the perspective of the archivist that has custody of it and from the records that document its provenance.

The one fact that raised eyebrows of the *Journal* readers was the change in the death date of the privateer. For over 120 years Texas and Gulf of Mexico historians commonly referenced the allegation that Jean Laffite died in 1824 (1825 or 1826) off the coast of Yucatan during a hurricane. His journal establishes that he died on May 5, 1854, in Alton, Illinois, under an assumed name. If his death in the mid-1820s could be proven or even fairly well established, the journal would become another type of mystery and the historians, writers, and Laffite enthusiasts could ignore it as a primary source, but the proof has not been found.

The Death of Jean Laffite

The tragic fate of this pirate king is told and retold by those who recollect the event. Just at a time when some of Lafitte's ships were away from the place of rendezvous, a strong force was set against him. He encountered it near Contoy and fought bravely but his ship struck a rock and sunk. He took to the boats with eight or ten men, and succeeded in landing on a sandbank called Blanquilla, but was pursued and surrounded. One by one his men fell; still he refused to surrender, and was killed there, defending himself as long as there was breath in his body.[2]

This 1886 version is but one of many tales recorded on Jean Laffite's death. The earliest notation that I found in the historical record dates from 1836, but it was recorded by Mirabeau B. Lamar on June 10, 1855 as information received from James Campbell at an interview at Galveston Bay. Campbell, a colleague of Laffite's, swore that in 1836, William Cochran, Laffite's first Lieutenant stated:

Lafitt sailed to the Southard and made the Cape Cartouch dividing the Honduras and Mexico, met a large ship and made up to her for action. She had 14 guns and made a sever fight; LaFitte was badly wounded in the action and lost several men. He captured her; and after holding her twenty-four hours, the supercargo ransomed her for one hundred thousand dollars, her cargo being estimated by the invoices at three times that sum. Cochran, being first Lt., Lafitt put him in command of the capture vessel as prizemaster. Lafitt and Cochran now ran to Vera Cruz [sic] and ran off an on waiting for the ransom, which was to be paid in twenty-four hours. . . . And a sever wound inflicted on LaFitt himself . . . Lafitt beat up to Venezuela, where he died of his wounds." Lamar indicated that Campbell thought the year to be either 1821 or 1822.[3]

In 1857 J. H. Kuykendall compiled his "Recollection of Early Texas" that was included in the Austin Papers. Kuykendall related the recollections of Judge Thomas M. Duke:

"In the year 1841" said Judge Duke "while I was collector of customs at Pas Cavallo, an old Portuguese sailor lived with me for some time. He said "Lafitte went from Merida to the Indian village of Celan(?) where he died. His old follower attended him in his last illness and after seeing the remains of his beloved commander interred in the Campo Santo of Merida, went to Honduras. The old sailor did not remember the year of our Lord in which Lafitte's death happened. "[4]

Kuykendall recorded that Judge Duke thought the year was either 1825 or 1826.[5]

William Bollaert penned in February-March of 1842 at Galveston, Texas:

He cruised about for a short time in the Gulf, went to the Island of Margarita near the Orinoco and reported to have died in Uycatan in 1826. Although there is no very positive information relative to him after that period, it is generally supposed that he died some years afterward there or in one of the West Indian Islands.[6]

On Saturday, January 15, 1843 William Bollaert added: "General LaMar tells me that after Lafitte left Galveston there are no authentic records concerning him, but it is probable that he is dead."[7]

This is in essence the extent of the primary historical record that documents Jean Laffite's death in either 1821 or 1826 at a number of places. By 1855 the history books established his death as illustrated by the following example: "Lafitte and Cochrane still continued to cruise against Spanish Commerce for some years . . . He died in Silan, a town of Ucatan, about fifteen miles from Merida, in 1826, and was buried in the Camp Santo of that place."[8]

John Henry Brown wrote that Laffite left Galveston on his ship The Pride with "his favorite Lieutenant, Wm. Cochrance," continuing their attacks on Spanish shipping until 1826. "In 1822 Lafitte visited Charleston, South Carolina. He made occasional visits to the port of Sisal, in Yucatan, and the island of Margarita, near the mouth of the Orinoco River. It is said that he died in 1826, at Sisal, a town situated about thirty miles from Merida, and lies buried in the Campo Santo of that town."[9] Joseph L. Clark cautiously and properly wrote in the 1939 Texas textbook: "They [Lafitte brothers] remained there [Galveston Island] until 1821, when they aroused the displeasure of the United States, whose navy set them wandering, never to be heard of again."[10]

The hearsay became fact and no one seriously challenged this notion until the 1950s when the Jean A. Laffite Collection became available to several writers and an English translation of the journal was published. Authors, especially popular and newspaper writers, have stated over the years that there is a marked grave and record of his burial in Yucatan and yet, no record of Jean Laffite's death or burial on the Yucatan peninsula can be found or documented.

Many researchers have sought proof of a grave or a burial at Yucatan.[11] The most auspicious evidence was found by Laffite Society member Dorothy McDonald Karilanovic when she received a response by Anthropologist Dr. Michel Antochiw on August 22, 1995 from Merida, Yucatan. Dr. Antochiw wrote: "It appears that in November of 1821 Pierre Laffite [Actually the official 1821 record states "Don" Pedro Lafit was interred November 10, 1821, buried in Dzilam, Yucatan.] was brought dead to the port of Dzilam, and was buried there."[12] He added that Miguel Molas, a former Laffite accomplice turned anti-contraband official on the Island of Mujeres, fatally wounded Pierre during a confrontation. Over the years, the Gulf waters washed away the cemetery leaving no trace.

In his letter Dr. Antochiw contended that much contradictory and false intelligence was previously disseminated, but Rubio Mane's collection, lost since 1937 until Antochiw located them in a private library in 1995, offers legally trustworthy information since the testimony in the document on Pierre's activities, death, and burial was taken from sworn witnesses before local Spanish officials. The Cultural Institute of Merida, Yucatan, Mexico published the complete report in January 1995.[13]

Dr. Antochiw declared: "In many texts, Jean is confused with his brother. The information known up to the present refers exclusively to Pierre."[14] This is the only record or notice of an official burial that comes close to any Laffite, and even this record is not 100 per cent reliable as to the death of Pierre.

Bethany Enald Bultman wrote in 1994 in *New Orleans*: "Theories regarding Jean Lafitte's final resting place flow as freely as beer on St. Patrick's Day."[15] This statement summarized the search of the historical and written record.

John Andrechyne Lafitte

In the 1940s a man by the name of John A. Lafitte[16] began his inquiries about his ancestor, his great-grandfather Jean Laffite. According to the chronicle, after retiring from the Missouri Pacific Railroad, John A. opened several trunks left to him by his grandfather Jules, who had died in 1924. Jules was like a father to him due to his own father's death when John was five years old. Unfortunately, the bulk of the documents and books were in French and

John A. was not certain what he had inherited from his family since they seldom spoke of its history. He knew that they descended from the Gulf pirate and that the "trunk archives" including the journal documented this fact. John A. dreamed of fame and fortune based upon this fortunate heritage.

He began contacting people about the value of these documents and utilizing the fame of Jean Laffite. Ray and Sue Thompson were possibly the first to meet John A. Lafitte when he contacted them in New Orleans in 1942 or 1943. "When we first met him (he was a guest in our home for a week) in 1943, he knew very little about Jean Laffite and seemed mainly interested in finding Laffite treasures. Because his story of being a Laffite descendant was so intriguing we rolled out the red carpet for him as we sincerely hoped he was. . . ."[17] The Thompsons shared information and introduced him to Lyle Saxon, Tulane University and Louisiana State University history professors, A. E. Parson and Dr. Gaylord Taylor.[18]

John A. told them he was a retired railroader, potentially traveling anywhere on railroad passes, and had all the time in the world to pursue his search. The Thompsons noted his eccentric personality which caused some suspicion on their part. "He was illiterate but very shrewd and wily—eccentric, bombastic, paranoic [sic] and easily alienated if you did not agree with him." With John A. promising to share his treasure of documents, the Thompsons continued contact until 1963 when they finally grew weary of him, concluding that he was a fraud.[19]

Notary Public Ethel MacAdow on May 13, 1947, in Atchison, Kansas, certified a birth information sheet, the only official record that has surfaced to document John Andrechyne Lafitte's birth and heritage. Based upon family bible records, this notarization recorded that he was born June 4, 1893, at Omaha, Nebraska; a son of Leon Jean Lafitte, born in the State of Louisiana on March 10, 1865, died on April 16, 1898. Leon was a son of Jules Jean Lafitte, born in Baltimore, Maryland on April 4, 1834, died October 10, 1924 in St. Louis, Missouri. Jules Jean was a son of Jean

Laffite and Emma Hortence Mortimore; Jean born on April 22, 1782 in Port-au-Prince, Haiti, died on May 4, 1854 in Alton, Illinois. Since he was born in 1893, it would have been fairly common to have a birth information sheet notarized in order to prove one's age for a delayed birth record, for social security purposes or for retirement plans[20].

On March 6, 1948, officials of St. Louis suggested to John A., a resident of Kansas City, that he contact Charles van Ravenswaay, the Director of the Missouri Historical Society in St. Louis, to follow up on his historical inquiries.[21] He wrote to Dr. Ravenswaay on June 19 remarking that he had "many letters on file from investigators, and newspaper writers since I gave photo stats to Galveston Texas Public Library" and thanked him for his letter of June 9 that included copyright blanks and other forms. Stating that he wanted to verify information about his grandfather and the location of St. Louis streets and cemeteries, he explained that " . . . My ancestor never used name Sylestor Lafflin. He used name: John Lafflin." and " I can only donate the manuscript material . . . "[22]

Their contacts and correspondence continued for several years until Ravenswaay received a letter on November 21, 1951, from Clyde H. Porter. Porter told the following story about John A. related to him from a friend, Frank Glenn.

"Four years ago a railroad employee named John Lafeitte [sic] came to the Cuban representative here in Kansas City asking if there is any way of checking Cuban port records to find the coming and going of certain ships about a hundred and forty years ago. After several months of this sort of thing he proposed that Mrs. Espinoza [sic] the Cuban's wife, translate a manuscript for him and get it published, they to divide any profits. This has been done and Glenn has the book to publish . . . The book purports to be the autobiography of Jean Lafeitte, the pirate, written when he was an old, old man living at Alton, Ill., under the name of Lafflin. It fits together perfectly. Glenn feels if it is a true autobiography, it is a find of the century . . . On the other hand Glenn feels it cannot possibly be anything but a fake and don't know what to do about it . . . Now for the bad parts—The owner is a freak who will not allow anyone to know where he lives and moves every three months—he still fears the wrath of the British. He is known to be a collector of old paper. He visits old bookstores trying to buy end papers from hundred year old books they are tearing up for one reason or another. He has hidden the original Book and will not again produce it . . . I forgot to say that Glenn tried to find Lafeitte letters to compare with the manuscript and so far has not been able to find anything that was not presented to this museum or that library by this man John who owns the book."[23]

Ravenswaay and John A. fell out and by 1953 Charles Ravenswaay questioned the journal's authenticity.[24]

This was after Stanley Clisby Arthur wrote *Jean Laffite, Gentleman Rover* published by the New Orleans Harmanson Press in 1952. It was followed in 1955 by Doubleday & Company's *The Corsair, A Biographical Novel of Jean Lafitte, Hero of the Battle of New Orleans* by Madeleine Kent.[25] These two works based upon the "trunk archives" began the debate on the death of Jean Laffite and his life after leaving Galveston.

John A. continued to work with his family papers. On May 4, 1955, he sent samples to the Harris Laboratories in Lincoln, Nebraska, for testing of the paper and ink. Lewis E. Harris, Director, replied on June 2, 1955, that they were more than seventy-five years old.[26] On August 11, 1956, he contacted the Library of Congress. In a reply letter dated September 5, 1956, David C. Mearne, Chief of Manuscripts Division, Library of Congress wrote:

Dear Mr. [Blank] We have examined and now return, the leaf from an account book which you enclosed, in your letter of August 11. The paper compares favorably with other specimens of the early nineteenth century, the record could have been made in or about 1830. The small scrap which contains writing in French appears to be on paper of somewhat earlier manufacture.[27]

Vantage Press published *The Journal of Jean Laffite: The Privateer-Patriot's Own Story* in 1958, copyrighted by John A. Laffite. [*sic*] The introduction declared that "Writing, in French at home, or as he traveled about the country, he worked at the task from 1845 to 1850. This volume is a translation of that journal." This work was supposedly done by nuns in New Orleans for John A., but unfortunately the translation was thought to be inadequate since phrases and even paragraphs were left out.[28]

During the 1960s, John A. traveled to Florida, New Orleans and Galveston, making public appearances and visiting people as the great-grandson of Jean Laffite. He was thought to be very peculiar in personality, well liked by some and scoffed at by others. He alienated many people which led to the discounting of his claims about the family papers. Two fires, one at his house on December 8, 1959, and one at a Spartanburg television station in May 1960, damaged or destroyed the majority of his collection. Even those events became rather bizarre since John A. claimed to the newspaper reporter that he had lost gold doubloons that were melted in the house fire and he sued the television station for negligence. According to his wife, the house fire destroyed the majority of the family documents.[29]

In 1966 he arrived in Galveston for the pirate celebration and attempted to sell his papers to the Rosenberg Library. John D. Hyatt declined, stating that the purchase price of $10,000 was too high, but expressed a future interest in the collection.[30]

By the summer of 1969 the seventy-six-years-old John A. relocated to San Antonio and then Midland, Texas. He started contacting Texas dealers and others in order to sell his family collection since he desperately needed money. Offering a sale price of $1,000, Charles Hamilton of New York requested two slave order documents for his July 9 auction and wished to take the entire collection on consignment.[31] Richard Santos, from the Bexar Archives in San Antonio, informed William Simpson and Johnny Jenkins about an old man who had come to him with some papers. Santos had reviewed them and claimed, "It is the most astonishing thing I have ever seen, because some of the things in these papers could only be proven by things in my archives, and I can assure you nothing has been salted here." Santos also warned them that the old man was somewhat strange.[32]

Simpson, Jenkins and John A. met in Austin. Simpson recalled that "He [John A.] did not want to show us the original collection, but he had numerous photocopies of it which he was willing to display to us. I refused, saying I could not sell from a photocopy and would not buy from one." Jenkins and Simpson agreed to buy the collection for $15,000 with each paying half, but John A. refused Simpson's check, saying, "Mr. Santos sent me to this man, but I don't know you." Jenkins paid him in full and Simpson paid Jenkins for his half. The partners desired to sell the collection as a whole and Jenkins agreed to market it. About a year later, Jenkins had difficulty with his cash flow, and he sold his half and delivered the collection to William Simpson.[33]

William Simpson remembered John A. Lafitte as a "railroad man" with gnarled, coarse hands, "very curious and highly paranoid," who thought that many people including the Thompsons and Charles Hamilton wanted to steal his collection. "He was not a bookish man. He would have been incapable of faking the collection. He was not, by a stretch of the imagination, what we would call a 'literate' man."[34]

In 1970 William Simpson of Houston owned the Jean Laffite Collection and took it to New Orleans, the Louisiana State University and the Rosenberg Library. "They were highly skeptical of my collection and critical of John," remembered Simpson who was shown a *Time* article including a paragraph about Mr. Laffite being a mail fraud. "So I put my collection away thinking I might not have an authentic collection. For more than a year I never looked at the collection."[35]

On February 20, 1970, John A. Lafitte died in Columbia, South Carolina. According to his death certificate, he was a retired engineer from the Missouri Pacific Railroad and had been born on June 4, 1893, in Nebraska.[36]

Simpson's interest increased when he loaned the collection in 1973 to John Howells, a Houston Internal Revenue Service employee and pirate buff who was married to a Laffite descendant. Howells borrowed the *Journal* of Jean Laffite and began the process of comparing its signatures to known Laffite documents, and having the collection analyzed. By 1974 John Howells was completely convinced that the majority of the papers were original and genuine.[37]

At a meeting of the Harris County Historical Society on May 6, 1975, John Howells, had the journal and showed it to Joyce Calhoon, the first Sam Houston Regional Library and Research Center Director, and Miriam Partlow, a Liberty County historical author. They in turn mentioned this to former Texas Governor Price Daniel. Howells wrote to Miss Miriam Partlow on May 9, 1975: "Since you mentioned your nephew Honorable Price Daniel is interested in Jean Laffite, I have enclosed copies of some documents he might like to have in his files." In June Judge Daniel, an associate Justice of the Texas Supreme Court, expressed to Joyce Calhoon his desire for her to follow up their contacts. On his behalf, she spoke with William Simpson concerning an inventory. Simpson responded that "He will have Mr. Bill Burch, an assistant, get it in the mail immediately and will also give the Society the first refusal on the Collection."[38]

After an inspection at Simpson's Houston Galleries, William J. Burch on July 16, 1975, made the sale. "For value received I hereby sell and convey to Governor Price Daniel Sr. of Liberty, Texas, the entire Jean LaFitte Collection, purchased by me from William Simpson." The amount was $12,500.00.[39]

In their press release of June 9, 1976, the Texas State Library & Historical Commission announced that "Former Governor Price Daniel has purchased the hand-written 257 page *Journal* of Jean Laffite along with a rare collection of the buccaneer's family bible, albums, daguerreotypes, and a contract with his ship captains." The release went on to state that it was to be donated to the Sam Houston Center and that the first public display would be on June 16, 1976 for the Regional Bicentennial Dinner at Beaumont. Daniel loaned the journal and other items for display at the grand opening of the Sam Houston Regional Library and Research Center on May 15, 1977. The journal "was initially delivered in 1977 from [the] Institute of Texan Cultures in a very tightly secured exhibit case . . . "[40]

Why did Price Daniel purchase this collection? Jean Laffite interested him due to Laffite's activities in Southeast Texas including his assistance to the Napoleon Refugees in 1818 who had established Camp d'Asile on the Trinity River. Daniel saw the collection as a center piece that tied in nicely with the history of Southeast Texas that additionally conjoined with his personal interests.

The Jean Laffite Collection was donated to the Texas State Library and Archives Commission by Price Daniel on August 1, 1978. This donation includes: I. The original *Journal* of Jean Laffite, a 13"x8"x3" slightly burned leather bound volume, written in French, 257 pages; 2. Leather bound ledger book, 13"x3"x1.5"; 3. Two family bibles (1839, French, 1608-1912 family information and 1820 French, 1742-1932 family information); 4. Small leather bound copy book, dating from 1840, property of Julius Laffite containing information on David Crockett, Andrew Jackson and others. 5. Small leather bound book printed in 1850, containing newspaper clippings and other entries; 6. Photographs of family and friends dating from 1850-1900, twenty- one loose photos and a photo album; 7. A small 6"x8" portrait of Jean Laffite; 8. 1806 Laffite ship document; and 9. Large portfolio containing photographs used in Stanley Clisby Arthur's book, *Jean Lafitte, Gentleman Rover*. Mrs. Price Daniel donated on November 27, 1989, an additional 2.5 cubic feet of materials that included original documents from the purchase as well as research materials that her husband had collected on Jean Laffite. This included five circa 1840 paintings, folk art by Little, of Laffite family members including Jean, Emma Hortense and sons Glen and Jules and correspondence between John A. Lafitte, his wife and Audrey Lloyd and Lloyd's manuscript.[41]

In summary, the Jean Laffite Collection at the Center contains

four cubic feet of correspondence, documents, graphics, manuscripts, maps, photographs, publications and artifacts. Two types
of material are represented in the collection: original documents,
manuscripts, photographs and artifacts, 1806-1955 belonging to
Jean Laffite or Laffite family members; and a collateral collection
of correspondence, publications and other items dating from 1938
to 1985 pertaining to Jean Laffite, the Laffite family and to the
original materials noted above.[42]

Authenticity

When Price Daniel purchased the collection in 1975, he knew
that it was controversial since he told Howells: "I have kept up
with the *Journal* in a general way ever since Stanley Clisby Arthur
wrote his book, *Gentleman Rover*, in 1952."[43] But he was satisfied
by the reports from Harris Lags, the Library of Congress and Ralph
O. Queen, a nationally recognized handwriting expert and former
criminal investigator with a specialty in forgery. Daniel knew that
Charles Hamilton, the Rosenberg Library and others had attempted
to purchase the collection and he had received favorable opinions
from several individuals including Richard Santos, Lacie Lafitte
Sanders,[44] and writer Audrey Lloyd. He perceived that historians
continued to debate the significance of the journal, but never
dreamed of what would transpire. In 1983 when I became the
Sam Houston Center's Director, Judge Daniel stated to me that in
several ways, he wished that he had never bought the collection for
he did not have time to respond to the critics and it was never his
intention to be in the center of accusations.

The controversy has a long history and it started with Ray and
Sue Thompson in 1942. After days of discussion, John A. Lafitte
finally showed the family bible to the Thompsons and permitted
them to photostat the inscription and title page. Later the
Thompsons discovered that their bible photostat did not match
another Laffite bible.[45] Sharing her memories of those years with
Robert Vogel and Pam Grunewald in 1975, long after John A.

decided not to work with the Thompsons, Sue remembered that they often "speculated on whether or not we unwittingly contributed in some way to the terrible hoax that John Lafflin finally perpetrated." Their initial excitement died after years of frustrating contact and receiving false information, along with false hopes. The Thompsons often suggested to John A. that the collection was invaluable and that it should be donated to the Library of Congress or at least not be carried around in a suitcase. "Did we, by emphasizing how priceless such a diary would be—plant a seed in his devious mind that he cultivated and nourished over the years until he had gathered together everything he wanted to present as facts?"[46]

In 1951 when John A. Lafitte was working with Ravenswaay, Clyde H. Porter related Frank Glenn's story to Ravenswaay.. This added to the speculation on the journal's authenticity. By this time John had alienated many scholars and writers by his personality and by not sharing the entire collection at one time, a behavioral pattern he continued until his death. Of course these people were also attempting to profit through publishing or in Ravenswaay's case, soliciting a donation for his institution. The provenance of the material was questionable mainly due to the reported death of Laffite in Yucatan in 1826 and due to the personality of the man claiming to be John A. Lafitte.

Personalities abound not only in the life of Jean Laffite, but in the controversy surrounding the papers as well. Unfortunately, the majority of the figures had some personal financial stake in them. There were winners and losers, and in some cases John A. definitely used people to his own advantage which was not an endearing trait. Another factor was a great deal of hearsay which often was not confirmed or could not be confirmed. Speculation became fact and facts were often twisted.

Stanley Clisby Arthur had access to the entire collection and apparently thought it was authentic when he authored his book which was published in 1952.[47] Arthur made no attempt at distinguishing written copies of documents from original ones, and ignored the fact that part of the collection was not written by Jean

Laffite. He referred to it all as Jean Laffite's papers which caused many of the questionable documents to be referred to as forgeries in future years. They are not fakes, but they are not original Crockett or Jackson or Lincoln or Jean Laffite items either.[48]

John A. Lafitte, prior to the Vantage Press publication of the journal, had two tests done: one by the Harris Laboratory and one by the Library of Congress. The tests were supportive of the journal, but have an inherent problem since they were done in the mid-1950s and the results are not very scientific compared to today's standards. It is not clear what pages of the journal were analyzed or what tests were performed. One cannot dismiss them, but the results are not conclusive either.[49]

In 1962 Frances H. Stadler, Manuscripts Librarian of the Missouri Historical Society, addressing his archival and historical colleagues, issued a warning about the passing of fraudulent Laffite documents. Unfortunately, Stadler repeated the 1948 to 1951 Charles van Ravenswaay letters concerning John A. Lafitte and did not include the fact that Ravenswaay had attempted unsuccessfully to secure the collection for the Missouri Historical Society or that the information was eleven years old.[50]

By 1969 when the dealers were attempting to secure John A. Lafitte's lucrative business, few seemed to consider the documents to be forgeries, but they all agreed that, in the words of John H. Jenkins, "He is a very nutty fellow, to say the least."[51] Charles Hamilton, John H. Jenkins and William Simpson were all very enthusiastic about the collection. Charles Hamilton wrote to John H. Jenkins on July 28, 1969, that he "was glad to hear that you made such a marvelous acquisition."[52] On September 23, 1969, Charles Hamilton wrote to John A. Lafitte thanking him "very much for your letter of September 20, explaining the circumstances of your sale of Laffite's documents and my belief that they would bring a large sum at my sales." Hamilton closed the letter "With good wishes to you and the hope that I will be privileged to handle some Laffite documents in the near future."[53] Of course Jenkins and Simpson ended up being the purchasers.

William Simpson by 1971 was not enthusiastic about the collection due to the lack of Jean Laffite documents for comparative tests and the negative reception that he received from various quarters. John Howells decided to take on the project of authenticating the Jean Laffite *Journal* and spent several years doing so. First he located the Le Brave Document in the Federal Regional Archives in Fort Worth and then the Laffite documents in the Texas State Archive's Lamar Papers. Simpson and Howells hired Ralph O. Queen, "Examiner of Questioned Documents." Queen was a former criminal investigator, nationally recognized handwriting expert with forty years experience in criminal investigation especially in handwriting identification for the Houston Police Department, the State of Texas and the Federal Government and a member of the International Association for Identification. Queen reported to John Howells on September 27, 1974:

"Reference is made to two pages of handwriting dated 7 Oct. 1846 and 24 Sept. 1849, signed Jn Lafitte, removed at random from a journal in your possession . . . A detailed study has been made of these documents and comparisons have been made of the handwritings contained on other documents bearing handwritings that have been accepted as being known writings of Jean Laffite, commonly spelled Lafitte. Some of the documents used for comparative purposes was the Le Brave document, Federal Court case, #1440, used to convict Capt. John Desfarges, two Jn Laffite Letters to Gen. James Long in the M. B. Lamar Collection in the Texas State Archives, known as documents #19 and #24. Also various other writings.

These examinations and comparison revealed that there are many individual personal characteristics appearing in the handwriting on the pages from the journal that are identical with characteristics appearing in the known writings.

Due to these findings, it is my opinion that the author of the known writings was also the author of the writings appearing on the two pages of the journal."[54]

Queen examined the entire journal between June and September of 1974 when he removed the two pages for comparison and testing work. He found that one was written in iron oxide ink, its ferrous content permeating the paper, and the other in Gallnut ink, and that the journal's paper, a linen based type used before 1850, contained several types of water marks, none of which were on record with the Institute of Water Marks, one being a large Fleur-de-lis. Queen further reported that the ink "cannot be readily removed by washing the paper . . . Microscopic examination was found to contain identical characteristics of letter formation . . . No change in formation of letters, slant or pen direction: a, e, t, o, d, p ."[55]

Queen was the first and only forgery expert to compare the journal with known Laffite documents. He truly believed and reported the journal to be authentic and that the writing matched the known handwriting of Jean Laffite. Unfortunately, there are very few known documents with a good provenance which creates a fundamental problem, coupled with the fact that there is no death record of Laffite to prove the standard accounts of history.

During 1973 Robert Vogel, then a graduate student and later the editor of the Laffite Society quarterly and a recognized Laffite scholar,[56] began a correspondence concerning the journal's authenticity with Charles van Ravenswaay, Sue Thompson, and Charles Hamilton. The four agreed with their conjectures that the Laffite Collection was a forgery and became the leading critics. Unfortunately, much of this discussion, sometimes in public forums such as newspaper articles, was based on opinion rather than fact. Charles Hamilton wrote to Robert C. Vogel in 1974: "Your assumption that all . . . are forgeries is quite correct . . . I corresponded with John A. Laffite [*sic*] about five or six years ago, and he finally sent me several documents . . . which took only a glance to identify as a forgery. Later I read an article in *Time* or *Newsweek*——I forget which——about Laffite being involved in several crooked schemes.[57] This is far different from the Hamilton writing to John A. Laffite and John Jenkins. Sue Thompson continued this track when writing to Pamela Grunewald and state that Vogel was the source of their information and that "Ray and I knew Stanley Arthur well and disliked him."[58]

Thompson went on to explain John A.'s motive for the forgery was " . . . money. He did quite well financially from it—radio appearances, TV appearances, newspaper stories, etc. etc. John Lafflin was a very devious man—uneducated but wily.[59]

Having no reason to doubt the expert knowledge of Charles van Ravenswaay, Sue Thompson and Charles Hamilton or not to trust their written statements to him, Robert C. Vogel wrote to Pamela Grunewald that John Andrechyne Lafitte's behavior "is not proof, in itself, that the Journals of Jean Laffite are a hoax, but a careful examination of his public statements and private correspondence leaves me with no other alternative than to believe that he was up to some mischief."[60] Unfortunately, Vogel, Hamilton, Thompson and Ravenswaay utilized each other as their expert or reliable source on the "forgeries" when none of them were that knowledgeable about the complete story and by neglecting to relate their personal interests. None of them had seen the entire collection. In the vicious circle of noncredibility, hearsay was often repeated and stated as fact.

Only Robert C. Vogel had some intellectual honesty in this debate and he brought several important points to light including the fact that Pierre Laffite was often confused with Pierre Boit Laffite and other relations of Bayou Pierre, Desoto Parish, Louisiana, and that some of the documents in the Jean Laffite Collection at the Sam Houston Center are not what they are reported to be.[61]

On August 1, 1978, when Price Daniel gave the collection to the Texas State Library and Archives Commission, he included this phrase: "This gift includes translations of the material now being arranged by Donor and the publication rights of the book now being planned by Donor . . . "[62] This added to the confusion since people kept expecting a new publication which never materialized, and added to the rumors that gained momentum for the controversy.

On October 16, 1979, John Howells wrote to the Honorable

Price Daniel in regard to the new questions of authenticity raised by Robert C. Vogel and other critics. In the letter Howells acknowledged Daniel's desire to have another forgery expert examine the Laffite *Journal* to provide a second opinion. "Therefore, while in New Orleans, I contacted a professor at the University of New Orleans, who teaches courses in hand writing identification. Her name is Marian Bethancourt." Howells convincingly argued that "By having the University of New Orleans accept the *Journal* as authentic, all historians would have to acknowledge its authenticity and any possible question would be settled forever."[63] Daniel replied that unless the cost was prohibitive, Howells should hire this expert and the bill would be paid for the Atascosito Historical Society.[64] If Daniel would not have been such a busy man, he may have had second thoughts about this if he would have read the so-called expert's biography.

Mimi Bethancourt studied graphology in 1959 as part of her Loyola University course on art therapy. From 1970 to 1979 she provided entertainment at New Orleans conventions with Dragon Associates by analyzing handwriting and taught a graphology course in the University of New Orleans continuing education department. In 1979 she added to her resume the fact that she was "writing a book *Love Letters, love relationships and compatability as revealed in handwriting analysis*" and a member of American Association of Graphologists, and the New Orleans Chapter of American Graphologists."[65]

Ms. Bethancourt visited the Center on November 28, 1979, and on January 12, 1980, wrote to John Howells about her big plans since she "spoke with lots of people, several offers to do a book on the journal and forgeries." She expanded by explaining her vision of writing two books, one for the New Orleans tourist trade that would include graphological personality profiles, and the second on the "adventure of disproving the journals." After inviting Howells to be their project historian Bethancourt enhanced the request by stating that "Everyone at this end sees a big chance for it on the national market, even including movie and t.v. rights."[66]

On January 16, 1980, Price Daniel received a copy of this letter to Howells with Bethancourt's final report dated December 11, 1979. Bethancourt declared under oath that she compared the 1806 Laffite document the "250 page Journal" and two family bibles with the 1819 Le Brave document, submitting the documents to various graphological tests. She found that the 1806 document was true and authentic, but "The Journal and Family Bibles were found to have many discrepancies and are therefore not authentic." Even though Bethancourt's conclusion does not include this statement, Howells added in his cover letter "She says she was as convinced as Ralph O. Queen, until she examined the personal letters by John A. Lafitte, which Ralph O. Queen did not have an opportunity to do."[67] Needless to say, Price Daniel was not very happy with these results and Bethancourt's actions. He was also puzzled since she found part of the collection authentic.

To add confusion to this matter, the *Sunday Times-Picayune* of June 8, 1980, ran the following front page headline: "Lafitte: Pirate's Costly Journal May Be Only a Famous Fake." Clancy DuBos in his feature article, detailing the purchase of the journal by Price Daniel, its history and the ongoing controversy, stated that " A 258-page handwritten journal purportedly written by legendary privateer Jean Lafitte and valued at $75,000 is a forgery, according to a New Orleans handwriting analyst and other authorities." Quoting Bethancourt, DuBos informed his readers that the journal was "One of the biggest freehand forgeries in American history" and that she "estimated it took between 10 and 15 years to complete." He added that "Coincidentally, Mrs. Bethancourt's conclusions of forgery are also those of Charles Hamilton, a New York handwriting expert . . . "[68] DuBos did present a balanced article, but it definitely featured Bethancourt.

Price Daniel learned from the incident that graphology according to the dictionary is the study of handwriting especially for the purpose of character analysis and that Howells was incorrect in stating Bethancourt's credentials, especially her status at the University of New Orleans. This was another strange chapter in the history of the collection. Due to personal events in Price Daniel's life, he never resumed his quest to resolve the question of authenticity.

This was closely followed in late 1980 by the publication of the book by Charles Hamilton, *Great Forgeries and Famous Fakes, The Manuscript Forgers of America and How they Duped the Experts.* Chapter eight featured John A. Lafitte and indirectly the Sam Houston Center's collection with the beginning sentence: "There was a pen and a bottle of Waterman's's brown ink, plus a stack of inherited forgeries of Jean Laffite's and other historical figure's handwriting that created more havoc in the world than the pirate and his crew of cutthroats." The chapter continued in this vein and upon a careful reading, did not shed a great deal of knowledge or light on the Jean Laffite Collection. "While there is doubt that John Laffite personally forged the Journal and other fakes of the pirates, as well as the documents of Robidoux and Lisa and the letters of Lincoln, there can be little question that the forgeries of Jackson and Crockett originated from his pen."[69]

Hamilton's prose was primarily based upon statements given by Ray Thompson, Charles van Ravenswaay and Robert C. Vogel, whom he characterized as "probably the world's greatest expert on Jean Laffite" and as the primary source of his information.[70] This book only fueled the critics' fire and did nothing to resolve any of the conflicts. Hamilton's own account contains many discrepancies especially of his role in attempting to acquire the papers from John A. Lafitte. Hamilton wrote this chapter without examining the Sam Houston Center's collection and frankly, misquoted Robert Vogel.

Earlier on June 26, 1980, Robert C. Vogel wrote to Price Daniel: "The controversy over the so-called "Journals of Jean Lafitte" has interested me for the better part of the last decade." As the managing editor of *The Life and Times of Jean Laffite*, Vogel informed him that a future issue would feature an article on the journal's authenticity and his own research concerning the historical validity of the Laffite Papers.[71]

Inviting Daniel to write an article for this particular issue, Vogel expressed his view that "his personal opinion is that the Journal MS was composed as a hoax, probably sometime during the latter part of the nineteenth century." Challenging the journal on grounds of inaccuracy and fabrications, Vogel added that he had not addressed "the physical properties of the manuscript itself: nor am I willing to point an accusing finger at the peculiar John Andrechyne Lafflin, alias Lafitte, who some have sought to label a forger."[72]

From 1980 the Laffite researchers and enthusiasts continued the debate on the collection's authenticity. Reminding one of the blues song line, "people talk, but they just don't know," the majority of the discussion was based on hearsay, misinformation, and the total assumption that opinion, especially printed opinion, equals fact. The known facts are often disregarded and there are numerous theories that have been proposed as to the journal's author.

The journal has had and does have many supporters over the years. Recent examples include Laffite Society member Dr. Reginald Wilson, who has spent several years poring over the entire collection and authored a 1996 paper in which he examined the handwriting and found it to be authentic, not like John A.'s; and long-term researcher Pam Keyes who wrote " . . . as I fully believe 90% of your Jean Laffite materials are authentic, and the proofs of their authenticity are readily at hand. Yes, even proofs that Robert Vogel would have to accept . . . "[73]

During their studies in 1996 and 1997, Pam Keyes and Dr. Reginald Wilson noticed a seal in the original journal at the end of Laffite's life story, only a privateer commissioned by Cartagena had such seals. It physically marked the change in the journal's subject for after it Laffite began his discourse on Karl Marx, governments, and philosophy. Is this as significant as it appears? Only further research will tell or answer this new mystery.[74]

In 1998 Robert Vogel summarized his position on the collection with the following statement:

Of course, much of the evidence supporting the charge of fraud against John Andrechyne Lafflin and his Journals of Jean Laffite is quite circumstantial in nature. I cannot prove beyond any reasonable doubt that the journals were written by anyone other than the real Jean Laffite—but I believe that I have proved conclusively that the *Journal of Jean Laffite: The Privateer-Patriot's Own Story* is filled with inaccuracies, inconsistencies and several glaring and outright distortions of the truth. I cannot show that Jean Laffite died in Yucatan in 1825 or '26—but I can question the reliability of the journal's account in the light of certain known facts regarding the character of Jean Laffite. Even if Jean Laffite did write his memoirs in Saint Louis in the 1840s—and I do not believe that he did— The *Journal* of Jean Laffite is at best a highly unreliable source of information on Laffite's role in American history during the turbulent years 1803-1830. The Journals of Jean Laffite must be disregarded in an objective and impersonal study of the life and times of Jean Laffite.[75]

As the Director-Archivist of the Sam Houston Regional Library & Research Center since 1983, I have had the privilege of being the custodian of the *Journal* of Jean Laffite and the Jean Laffite Collection. What is my opinion based upon twenty-three years of archival experience? The Jean Laffite Collection is typical of most family papers: it is a hodgepodge of documents including photographs that are identified only by the writing on their backs, newspaper clippings and other rather mundane material. The journal is not a crude forgery and appears to be authentic as does the rest of the collection. It does contain a wealth of information that cannot be readily found in other primary sources. There is no doubt that some people including John A. Lafitte and the dealers claimed that parts or certain documents were authentic when they were not originals, but copies made by some family member or perhaps even written by John A. Lafitte.

Only one forgery expert to date, Ralph O. Queen, has examined the *Journal* of Jean Laffite and he concluded that it was authentic. There are no credible studies to prove that the *Journal* is a forgery, but there is no positive proof of what it claims to be either.

It appears to be authentic and as an historian, I would see it in that light with caution due to its provenance as I would any other manuscript especially a self-serving autobiographical account. There is no proof that John A. Lafitte forged a single document.

In conclusion, historians do have the right to be skeptical of the *Journal* of Jean Laffite as they should be of any source that has a strange provenance, but they should not totally dismiss the Jean Laffite Collection. There is no doubt that the paper and ink of the journal should be tested utilizing the most modern methods by a totally independent party and this would be the first step in the right direction. The results of such a test could end the debate. Unfortunately, this does require funds, estimated at $15,000 several years ago, which is more than the collection was purchased for in 1975. Is this the responsibility of the Texas State Library and Archives Commission as custodian of the documents? In an ideal world it would be, but when considering the other holdings at the Sam Houston Center, over 16,000 cubic feet, and the vast commission holdings in Austin, it is not a high priority. One could argue that it would not be a prudent investment of tight resources when considered with all of the other budget items.

The Sam Houston Regional Library and Research Center does have the obligation to continue to collect any information on the *Journal* and its controversy in order to make the information available to its researchers. It is the Center's obligation to inform researchers that the *Journal* of Jean Laffite is not a proven forgery that should be dismissed outright and there is a body of literature that is highly critical of it.

In March 1999, Robert Vogel and I discussed the many possibilities of the journal's origin and the fact that even if the tests proved beyond any doubt that it was from the correct time period, it would not end the controversy. We agreed, based on our research, that it seemed highly unlikely that John A. Lafitte could have forged the French journal. We concluded the following possible scenarios: 1. The journal is indeed the work of Jean Laffite; 2. The journal is a forgery and a fraud; 3. The journal was written by a family member or a friend or former associate familiar with the life of Jean Laffite as a potential novel based upon discovered family papers which are part of the collection. These were in turn found or inherited by John A. Lafitte; 5. The journal could have been composed in the nineteenth century as part of that era's tide of romantic pirate literature and been found by John A. Lafitte. We could have speculated for hours since it is impossible to prove a negative.

The Jean Laffite Collection and the sources utilized in this introduction are open to all researchers. While normally on exhibit, the *Journal* of Jean Laffite, due to the fire damage, is too fragile for researchers' use, but an excellent photo copy is available.

Charles Ramsdell, Jr. wrote in his 1940 article, "Why Jean Lafitte Became a Pirate," "Jean Lafitte belongs to folklore rather than to History . . . "[76] Perhaps he is correct.

TRANSLATOR'S NOTES

Translations are inevitably inadequate. The manuscript of the *Journal* attributed to Jean Laffite presents special problems because of its condition. In addition, there are the challenges of fidelity to the author in style and meaning, of the English-speaking audience, and of the existence of an earlier translation which demands justification of the effort to present a new English version of what is in fact a memoir rather than a journal.

As the manuscript now at Sam Houston Regional Library and Research Center was damaged in a 1960 fire, the original translators of the *Journal* had the advantage of a more complete text. Damage is mostly limited to the top lines of pages and ranges from a few letters to the entire line. By using context and a remaining letter or two it was possible to reconstruct many lines. When nothing was left, I turned in recourse to the 1958 translation. In one instance the missing line was also absent from the old translation, and it was necessary to construct a line from what came before and after the lacuna. Because of this problem there will never be an absolutely authentic and accurate translation of the once-complete manuscript.

Even without the effect of the fire there are problems for any translator of the *Journal*. The text, which has no erasures or cross outs, has missing words, misspellings, and repeated words, and in other places there are sentences that are incoherent. The translator must correct what are obvious errors and attempt to either make sense of apparent nonsense or leave it out of the translation. When I could guess at a logical meaning, I forced it upon the text. In cases where the meaning would not come out of hiding or was hopelessly ambiguous, the translation is followed by a [sic]. The reader will also find additional use of the [sic] when the original makes statements that appear factually or logically questionable to the translator.

Another problem in the manuscript is its mundane style. For the most part, that style appears in the translation. A translation must never be and can never be truly literal, but a paraphrase of the original becomes more like a plagiarism of original ideas than an attempt to reproduce them with some accuracy. A personality emerges from the words used by the author of the *Journal* to express his ideas, and in the same sense his syntax also expresses the man. When it is practical to do so, that syntax and those words are respected in the translation even when a certain clunkiness results.

At the same time, it is important to note that ideas and not words are translated. In some instances I followed the author's word choice precisely. He used *vaisseau* rather than *bateau, navire,* or *bâtiment* for ship, and I respected that choice by using "vessel" in the translation. At other times, a word translated from French to English has several possible choices, each with its own nuance; in those cases I attempted to match tone, meaning, and readability for an English-speaking audience. I also compromised between the original punctuation and my own interpretation of standard English punctuation with the resultant hybrid, which should satisfy no grammarian but, I hope, preserves some of the flavor of the original while restoring readability.

The challenges just mentioned already give a partial justification for a new translation of the *Journal.* In addition, there are 35 omissions of letters, words, or sentences in the 1958 translation and 141 errors of translation or transcription in the same book. Allegedly, six people worked on the first translation, and there is a variation among those translators ranging from almost literal fidelity to the text to what amounts to an English summary of the original French. There are some places in the original manuscript that are truly ambiguous, and sometimes the new translation has an alternate but no more certain choice in the interpretation of those ambiguous meanings. At other times word choices are arbitrarily and coincidentally different between the two translations. Neither choice is necessarily better than the other.

The inaccuracies of the original translation, however, justify a new translation, which, it is hoped, will find a wider audience than the 1958 *Journal,* while providing further fuel for the fires of the never-ending debate about Jean Laffite and his life beyond the confines of the official historical record.

ACKNOWLEDGMENTS

I owe thanks to many individuals who have helped me bring to light this new translation of the *Journal* signed with the name Jean Laffite. My department head, Dr. Joe Cash; Dean of Liberal Arts, Dr. Millard Jones; Vice President of Academic Affairs, Dr. Jim Brown; and Dr. Robert Hebert, McNeese State University President, all made special effort to help me obtain a sabbatical leave to do the transcription and translation of the manuscript. Thanks also go to Robert L. Schaadt, Director Archivist of Sam Houston Regional Library and Research Center and Ms. Darlene Mott of his staff, both for their help in getting access to the original manuscript in Liberty, Texas, and for Mr. Schaadt's scholarly introduction to this new translation.

Dr. Tom Watson of Lake Charles, Louisiana, originally introduced me to the manuscript and its mystery, and Dr. Reginald Wilson of Dayton, Texas, has provided me with both material and moral support, as have the members of the Laffite Society headquartered in Galveston, Texas. Of course, the most moral and editorial support has come from my wife Bettie, and I hope to spend many more years thanking her for her help, forbearance, and love.

Gene Marshall

FOREWORD

Since my retirement as an advocate for others a few years ago, due to my present age, I have been constantly encouraged to prepare a journal in which I shall lay down a complete narrative on the following pages so that I may of my free will and good faith leave my descendants a confidential account, which they must not release before the long period of 107 years has gone by from this present date.

For several months I have refused to reveal my past, which is completely private and concerns no one other than myself. If my records were missing, I am afraid that I would not be able to write the facts about the events in detail, just from memory, so as to avoid exaggeration.

The manner in which I shall begin to write these accounts will doubtless lead me to undertake several years of adventure, to compile adequate evidence of authenticity so, consequently, I shall not be afraid, but I hope that my notes will be adequate to the task of confounding the scheme of degenerate writers in the distant future of dwelling upon fairy tales about me and, at the same time, will avoid intensifying such presumptions into enduring legends.

YOUTH

I was of raw material in my childhood, and from that was I made.

My mother died before I can remember her, and my maternal grandmother lived so intimately with us that she became a mother for me. Grandmother knew instinctively that a child, from its birth, is formed by the impressions that it receives and that the family's example would be a determining factor of my upbringing.

Grandmother and the house we lived in then, made up the only world that I knew at the time when I learned to speak and acquire the habits that are necessary to the development of a strong personality ready to confront with a firm, determined will all the vicissitudes that life reserves for us, along with a capability of ignoring all that could hinder the development of my mind.

My first memories at the age of three were of an iron pot, and my next memory was the sight of oxen pulling a plow. At the age of five my first gifts were a leather harness and a little terrier from my father. My following presents were from my grandmother: a quill pen and scissors for drawing and cutting.

My grandmother was of Spanish and Jewish heritage. Her very liberal mind allowed her to make herself obeyed more by recourse to reason than to feelings. She never raised her voice, and because of that I learned from my childhood to control my voice and elocution so as to express my thoughts with calm and confidence.

When I was six, my grandmother began to teach me to spell in Spanish. When I was eight, Madame Raquel Seguria was my teacher of arithmetic, history, geography, and grammar. At the age of 12 Mr. Jn Christophe Chauterys was my teacher of navigation and maps. When I was 14, my brother Pierre and I were sent to Martinique to continue my studies. The Cruger Brothers taught

us. When we had finished studies at our private school, we went to
the island of Saint Croix to take courses in psychology to acquire a
better understanding of human nature.

We took courses in military preparation on the island of Saint
Christophe to learn swordsmanship, navigation, and artillery marks-
manship. Upon returning to Port-au-Prince, we learned the art of
fencing and dueling with masters of arms who taught us the secret
principles of that art.

My father had engaged in the trade of leather, working both
in Spain and France, and in Morocco he had learned the secret
processes of tanning hides before he emigrated to Port-au-Prince,
located on the island of Santo Domingo where I was born. My
paternal grandfather had also been a leather worker in France. Later,
because of religious persecutions that were then taking place, his
properties were confiscated, and his family was forced into exile
and forced to go live near the Swiss frontier.

My mother's father had been an alchemist with a good clien-
tele in Spain. He was a free-thinking Jew without Catholic faith
and without any traditional adherence to Jewish synagogues, but
he met a sad end. He died from malnutrition for having refused to
give up all the technical details that the authorities demanded
during an Inquisition against the Jews.

Grandmother never lost an opportunity to tell me about all
the tribulations her relatives were subjected to at the time of the
Spanish Inquisition, which held sway then, and that many persons were imprisoned for life and others had to seek exile.

My forebears were taught to expect and receive affection and
attention. Every effort was made to minister to their needs and to
make them feel an important part of the family and to discourage
any feeling of inferiority among them.

Many descendants of my ancestors who were persecuted now
live in the countries of Central Europe, where they are considered
among the best diamond cutters in the world; they have also gained
the reputation of having been skillful enough to create an atmo-
sphere of peace, contentment, and true happiness around them.

My grandmother's stories and the horrible sights to which I was later witness when the Spaniards smuggled weapons to the black slaves for their rebellion against the French who lived in the west of Santo Domingo, now called Haiti, caused me to learn to hate the Spanish crown and all the persecutions for which it was responsible, not only against the Jews but also against the poor ignorant people of any race, including its own subjects, who were deprived of our grandmother and did not receive the same good education that my brother Pierre and I had. My brother Pierre had also learned the same stories from my grandmother. As for me, I was the youngest of eight children, with four brothers and three sisters. Pierre, who was exactly two and a half years older, and I naturally felt very close, and our speculations and views on any subject were alike.

Alexandre our eldest brother was busy being a sailor at sea. He was 11 years my senior and had little to do with our family life. Marcus was nine years older than I. Henri was seven years older. Marcus and Henri were the kind who do not talk very much, and they did not learn easily. They worked more with our father in his leather shop, which was once located in the heart of Port-au-Prince.

During my childhood Port-au-Prince was a splendid, very lively city surrounded by magnificent plantations and resplendent with all kinds of tropical flora. A little later, during my adolescence, the city was completely destroyed during the insurrection of the slaves and the massacres that took place in the entire island of Santo Domingo, a part of which is now called , as I said before, Haiti.

We all received a good education, being taught by tutors who held classes in private homes. My brother Pierre and I were the youngest of the family, and we burned with the desire to learn how it would be possible to shake off the despotic yoke of Spain and make freedom prevail over all of Spanish America.

The smuggling and duplicity of the Spaniards caused Henri Christophe and Toussaint l'Ouverture to execute my countrymen.

My brother Alexandre would arrive from time to time from his sea voyages to stay a few days. My brother Pierre and I always

wanted to share the same bedroom as Alexandre, who kept us awake
until close to midnight as he told us the stories of his trips to
Cuba, Mexico, and South America. He told us about the strange
customs of the natives of those countries, the majority of whom
were forced to load ships with merchandise of all kinds as well as
with metals like copper, silver, and gold, all of it intended for their
Spanish masters. We were fascinated by all he told us and gradually we began to want to become sailors, too.

At a time when we were still very young, Pierre and I left our
school to take courses in a private institution that taught navigation. Because all the great schools of navigation were in France, so
far from us, we decided that our great uncles Antoine and Felix,
the brothers of our grandmother, would be our teachers. During
their military service they were decorated artillerymen, like our
brother Alexandre, who also knew how to make powder and tem-
per steel.

Alexandre was a good soldier and an expert cannoneer on a
vessel at sea. He was short with a curved nose and big eyes, which
were always lively and alert to the least noise or movement. We
had never seen any Jews in our community, nor knew how they
appeared, but our grandmother told us that Alexandre and our
sister Anna and brother Marcus had Jewish features. Alexandre
had a great interest in us, and he was very generous, and he always
had good stories to relate; sometimes, however, at the least provo-
cation he got angry.

He always brought numerous objects from his privateering
voyages under the orders of Captain Jn Puilijon. Alexandre always
invited Captain Puilijon to come to the house when they were in
Port-au-Prince, and I remember quite well that I was five and Pierre
eight when the captain came to our house for the last time. We
kept asking him to tell about his latest adventures, and it is almost
impossible to imagine all the dangerous moments that filled his
memory or the incredibly unjust manner with which he was treated
by the American Colonial Congress in Washington. [sic]

Despite his nonchalant attitude, his cold stare and livid lips told how greatly grieved he was when he asserted that, to him, the members of that Congress were only gibbet birds, and that he preferred to be hanged rather than set foot again on the American coast. "No, a hundred times no," he would say repeatedly, "I have been around the American coasts for too long; from today hence no more foreign land for me, a hundred times no!" Captain Puilijon's last visit to the house lasted three days and two nights; upon his departure, he told us that he planned to take a post in the Russian Navy.

Captain Puilijon told us all that he knew about the sea and how he conducted his privateering activities against the English, whom he had always hated and worked against in many ways. He told us among other things that the English, the French, and the Americans had not yet been able to discover either his true identity or the place of his birth, whereas he was born in Guadeloupe of a French father and a Scottish mother. Captain Puilijon advised my Uncle Reyné and my brother Alexandre never to reveal their real name or origin when they plied the trade of privateer for or against countries at war.

When I saw him for the last time, at the moment of his last departure, I really understood that those whom he had helped to establish American freedom, with his own privateering vessel and without receiving anything in return, had completely forgotten him. I was still but a child at that time, but the explanations that Uncle Reyné and my brother Alexandre gave me of the discussion that had taken place during the last visit of Captain Puilijon were enough to fill my memory with thoughts that still make by blood boil and still put me in the impossible position of pointing out my right to say that, for a certain time, I did everything to save the same nation from complete annihilation so as to preserve its freedom, based on that most sacred document: the Declaration of Independence, without receiving any compensation for it.

Jean Laffite

Ann Arbor, Friday, August 8, 1845

Alexandre did not sail under any other captain since Captain Puilijon bid us farewell in route to a foreign country. Alexandre, who was at the house most of the time with much leisure time, had a gift of telling sea stories, which filled our heads. Pierre and I considered such visions and desires to be prophetic glimmerings of a destiny we felt we had to fulfill. Our father never directly opposed Alexandre when he taught us the customs and the duties of a privateer against warring nations.

Grandmother, upon whom Pierre and I relied, however, never said anything to us either about Alexandre or his intention of becoming a privateer himself. She made him hush every time he would relate in front of us one of his privateering stories in which the crew was thrown into the sea when the ship was captured.

To hide our true intentions we had to leave the greater part of the realization of our desires in Alexandre's care when he was back on land. Yet, all those difficulties only made our determination grow. We had decided to do all that was necessary when we were grown so that we could capture ships flying the Spanish flag.

About six and a half years after the departure of Captain Puilijon, Alexandre was 22 and wore a little mustache. He undertook the repair and fitting of a brig as a privateer's ship. It was an old hull, good at most for coastal navigation on a calm sea, but he did the impossible. The vessel had two masts and four excellent cabins.

The first time out, Alexandre decided to embark his crew only after nightfall, then to raise anchor without delay and secretly make sail under a good, favoring breeze. The brig set sail at midnight with Alexandre as captain with a crew of nine men and a month's provisions, ammunition for six small cannons, muskets, and swords. Our father was the only person who followed him to the pier, and he heartily laughed at the boasting of Alexandre that no ship at sea could surpass his brig.

The next day Pierre and I jumped out of bed to hear our father tell the important story of Alexandre and his midnight departure on the high sea with a sloop, all sails flying, rigged like a brig with a half-forecastle. There was a heavy wind, and it was very cool as our father continued to coldly say, however, that he knew Alexandre had indulged in a foolish caprice and he greatly doubted that Alexandre was still alive at that moment.

I can hardly say what I felt upon hearing the pessimism of my father concerning Alexandre's venture, but as soon as he said the words I had a shiver of agitation and pleasure and the thought that Alexandre's "foolish caprice" was one of the most reasonable and even charming things in the world. Days passed, and then weeks, without word or sight of Alexandre's brig in the port. We asked our father about the route that Alexandre had planned to take and when he thought Alexandre would return to port.

All our father wanted to say was that Alexandre whistled for a few minutes and sang while raising the jib and the main sails and said, "I'm going to sea, without fear, to capture a great prize. Farewell, my Father." There was something in the tone of my father's words the next day that struck a terrible feeling of terror in our hearts. Pierre and I began to think that not everything was going well for Alexandre, who had been at sea for over a month. Our grandmother always kept a complete silence regarding Alexandre and his skill as a privateer. Pierre and I always gave in to her because of her great intuition and her good convictions, and we decided to withstand everything with great fortitude, having great faith in Alexandre's ability to return one day.

Eight weeks had gone by, and Pierre and I had reconciled ourselves to the opinion and calm resolutions of our grandmother when, unexpectedly, a French captain arrived in port to give us news of Alexandre's brig, which had a fire at sea returning from New Orleans. I shall never forget the intense anguish that I suffered at that moment. Our grandmother remained very calm, betraying neither emotion nor alarm.

Pierre and I left immediately to run to the pier by the sea. We jumped over all the flowers and between the banana stalks, trip-

ping each other up, impetuously falling down, as we hurried to
the pier to learn the news, to see if the story of Alexandre's misfor-
tune recounted by the French captain was true.

That day the wind, which was more and more frightening,
came from very far out at sea and doubled to break against the
dock. Pierre and I had scarcely spent half an hour at the dock
when, on the horizon, we saw two ships that were approaching the
port's dock. Several men were on lookout waiting for the vessels,
which drew near the port; they talked about who would be at the
helm of the larger ship. A few of the men remained at the steering
stern posts, singing melodious songs as the larger ship advanced,
coming still closer to the port.

The larger arrived first and was fastened and attached to the
dock posts. Next, the second ship, after several difficult efforts
made while zigzagging, worked itself close enough to raise its chain
anchors and, coming closer, maneuvered to within range of the
dock's posts.

The second ship was a very big Dutch-built brig, painted black,
with a showy, gilded, somewhat battered and broken figurehead,
that appeared to have gone through some very strong storms at
sea. A few manacled sailors who looked like Dutchmen were lying
on canvas sails near the starboard under the bowsprit. They looked
at us with great curiosity, and we decided that the majority of the
men we saw in manacles and chains on the two vessels were sailors
who had been captured and taken prisoners. Pierre and I went
very close to the vessels as soon as they had been fastened to the
dock posts without the rough dock workers, who were busy lowering the gangplank, seeing us. Pierre and I were very curious to
know how the vessels were going to unload the cargo.

The first man to go down the gangplank was wrapped in a sea
captain's deep red greatcoat, his face unshaven, with a red woolen
cap on his head. He spoke with a rough voice in various tones,
paying very little attention in such a strange way that it was not
easy to recognize him. As he came down the gangplank, his red
hat fell off his head, and we immediately recognized him as our

brother Alexandre. Pierre and I jumped up and poured out our souls with cries of thanks that he had returned, unexpected, but safe with his prize of two vessels.

Alexandre, however, allowed us only very little time for questions and comments, insisting that we go back to the house to our grandmother and saying that he did not have time to talk at the moment but that he was returning to the house later to give a detailed account of his adventure and his two vessels captured as booty. He immediately went to the government office with an accounting of his captured cargo, leaving a subordinate captain in his employ with two assistants to guard his two vessels in the port.

The day after the arrival of Alexandre had been spent with the bank and government authorities who made an inventory record in order to convert his cargo's assets into currency. The cargo consisted of two small vessels and all the merchandise: big barrels of whale oil, barrels of wheat, bales of fiber, silk, linen, wool, tanned hides, and leather, Negro slaves, and many silver bars. The year, 1792, Alexandre was at the house for some time because he remained in Port-au-Prince for three weeks, as best I recall. Our grandmother always tried to change the subject when Alexandre talked to us in her presence about privateers who captured vessels and drowned their crews, giving her a slight suspicion that the scholars could be marvels of deception at home.

In a few days after the sale of the merchandise and slaves, Alexandre found himself both attracted and repelled in a very complex way by all those who anticipated the bracing effect of the little injection of money in the entire city and who made him offers of speculation in ships and plantations in the colonies to establish the basis of a great credit business. Alexandre was determined to eliminate any unpleasant impression from his thoughts so as to be generous, and he was always very careful in giving gifts.

In accordance with our deceptive plans for the future of not letting our grandmother know our intentions, Pierre and I had to leave many of the plans to Alexandre so that he would teach us about privateering. Our grandmother's opposition did not lessen our desire. On the contrary, it poured oil on the fire. Pierre and I were determined, at whatever cost, to continue with our projects, when we were men, to make plans, plans by which we intended to capture every ship that sailed under the Spanish crown.

After all the sales of ships and merchandise, Alexandre became interested in the prospect of an enormous venture arranged by some bankers to float a big loan to France since the French and the English had contended so much that vital commercial voyages were doing poorly because of the great British fleet. The struggle between France and England was going to be very long. Regular commerce was almost completely halted, but there was enough intermittent commerce to slip cargo through, since the fortunes of war varied a lot in the Gulf of Mexico and the Mediterranean.

French *assignats* disappeared completely and their equivalent, called *francs*, subsequently the currency for France, had to come from foreign sources.

Although it was the first time that Alexandre was the captain of a privateering vessel for himself, he was not very worried because he knew that he had a larger vessel, well-equipped with more cannons, and ready to set out to sea at any time.

Spain owned the province of Mexico—exploiting and milking it like a cow—and had all the gold and silver locked up in Mexico but was afraid to move it because of the English fleet operating in great numbers in the Atlantic Ocean. Because of that, Napoleon could overcome the difficulty with great ease.

For all those reasons, Alexandre's future appeared magnificent. First, his plan was to capture the English vessels and thus weaken their fleet, then later to attack the Spanish commercial fleet. Alexandre and our uncles on our mother's side had no scruples in regard to Spain or England, which they considered animals of prey.

While Alexandre's officers and crew prepared his large vessel for a new expedition, he received a large sum as well as a letter of marque and of credit for his subsequent privateering voyages without money concerns.

A good number of influential merchants secretly met close to where my father's shop was located to congratulate Alexandre and his crew for their courage. They christened his vessels *Bonheur* and *Succès*. It was strange to see how important they considered Alexandre after some expeditions where he showed himself to be a skillful privateer cannoneer; because of this he was received at dinner by the greatest names of France.

Pierre and I were still very young, and we imagined our future, based on one hand upon the experience of Alexandre, and on the other upon the intuition of Grandmother, who told us that my brother and I were destined to enlighten, with our pen, the throng of suffering men exploited by the brutes who ruled over them.

In any case, the intentions of Grandmother, who believed that by the power of our pens we would participate in the emancipation of suffering humanity, caused a crowd of thoughts to file through our poor heads and made us feel as though we were on the edge of an abyss. We had only one hope, that one day we would be able to strike a great blow, on the sea, against those two beasts: Spain and England.

When I was 16, my eldest brother Alexandre Frédéric and Pierre and our Uncle Antoine went to New Orleans, Louisiana, and returned to us at Port-au-Prince on January 19 after a three-month stay in New Orleans. Because of illness we stayed at home until March 1798. When I was 17, we left and took a ship for our country, New Orleans, and we encountered robbers who took all our belongings.

Pierre and I entered the privateering business as sailors for our passages. The first vessel confiscated by us was owned by a Spanish family from Santo Domingo that spent most of the time in New Orleans. We transported refugees and fugitives in an exodus far from Spanish domains, as well as from Port-au-Prince, which was inflamed with discontent from Spanish conspiracy.

Our brother Alexandre took Pierre and me along on several trips to the islands of Nevis and Saint Christophe during 1798; in September of that year he took us to the fortress of Cartagena. We met French, English, Danish, and Dutch sailors. Grandmother missed me very much, and she would cry more each time that I embarked aboard a vessel. Pierre and I were witnesses to the first human torture and executions under the Spanish regime in Cartagena; we returned to Port-au-Prince in November 1798.

I was 18 and Pierre 21 when Alexandre began his ninth year as a privateer; his experiences had hardened him and made him a brilliant man as well as a skillful cannoneer and an enthusiastic servant of France. He was 29 and still a bachelor when he decided to leave the Antilles and place himself at the disposition of Napoleon Bonaparte in Europe, leaving his six vessels under the command of three captains.

Pierre married Françoise Sel at the age of 19 and already had a son when Alexandre left for France. Two months after Alexandre's departure and when I was 18, I married Christine Levine on the island of Saint Croix; she was a Jewish woman of Danish ancestry.

Pierre and I, as well as our wives, wanted to taste a life of adventure, and we made several risky voyages to Cuba, Mexico, and Florida during which time we received confirmation of all our brother Alexandre and our uncles had told us. Those voyages, as well as my first some time later, confirmed us in our intention of being privateers.

Many things had changed in Santo Domingo during the French-English war, and for that reason we forgot the advice of our grandmother, who saw us as men of letters, preaching morality to humanity. Instead of the pen, Pierre and I decided to follow the example of our uncles and brother and take up the sword.

The English and Spanish had smuggled arms and powder to the slaves living in the western part of Santo Domingo, which some time later caused revolts that extended all over that territory and were the cause of many massacres and of the flight of those who could get out.

Jean Laffite

Detroit,
Monday, the first day of September, 1845

Although Alexandre was so far away, we had the feeling that we would soon be reunited in the goal of accomplishing more important things.

Pierre had two children after three years of marriage, and I myself had a son during the first year of my marriage. But, despite the pleasure that we gave our wives and the fact that we recognized they were slaves to their children, they made us understand the desire they had for their own home, a feeling that we too could not entirely repress. Our houses at Port-au-Prince were as nice and comfortable as our wives could desire. It was less difficult, therefore, to enlist under the command of Alexandre's captains, who commanded his vessels themselves under the orders of Uncles Reyné, Felix, and Clemente, who were the half-brothers of Grandmother and who had received from Alexandre the command of eleven vessels and their crews, comprised of 286 qualified men, consisting of cooks, rope makers, sail cutters, calkers, clerks, locksmiths, lieutenants, cannoneers, smiths, ship carpenters, and 45 slaves working at the docks.

Alexandre was in France from 1801 to 1804 and from 1805 to 1806. Pierre and I were old enough to serve as privateers under the orders of our Uncle Reyné.He had arranged everything, and that was possible despite the entreaties of Grandmother, who claimed that we were still too young to captain a ship on the high sea. Grandmother was close to 72, and I was almost 19 in the early spring of 1801 when we raised the sails on two vessels for a privateering run.

Uncle Reyné commanded a 350-ton vessel, and Pierre and I had received the command of a 300-ton vessel, which was to follow the vessel of Uncle Reyné, making sail toward the west in the direction of Trinidad and Cuba, then still toward the west and for two more weeks in the direction of the Yucatan.

Our two vessels sailed along the Yucatan coast without any

incident more important than the occasional encounter of Mexican mestizos on their fishing boats. However, at about the middle of April 1801, when we were in the region of Vera Cruz, we encountered very strong winds that carried one of the most violent storms we ever experienced. Happily, everything had been well-stowed in the holds before our departure, but our two vessels showed their good qualities, their prows under the water at each pitch and emerging with difficulty from under a wave only to be engulfed again by the next. The southeast wind gave us a lot of anxiety for several hours, forcing our vessels on the ends of their beams and the small sails forced to beat against the mast. As the wind diminished, we were fortunate enough to right our vessels without any injuries or loss of life or damage to the mast material, and, finally, we found ourselves in as good a condition as before the wind struck. Our Uncle Reyné thought that our escape was almost a miracle.

Wednesday, the twenty-second of April, exactly at daybreak, almost a week after the storm, as I well remember because it was my birthday, we sighted through our binoculars a very distant sail heading east on the horizon. Although the vessel could not have been at less than 25 kilometers distance and heading in the opposite direction from us, we immediately began with great effort to prepare our rigging and completely deploy our sails in order to sail east toward the vessel sighted.

As our vessels continued to go faster and shorten the distance between the vessel which continued toward the east, we immediately began signaling in all possible ways, flame-colored sails as high in the air as the masts allowed, and trying to gain their attention with cannon fire, but, of course, the vessel kept sailing, thinking that we were privateers. They were afraid we would seize the vessel loaded with cargo, which would be a great prize to capture. Uncle Reyné, in our large vessel, continued to sail ahead as all the men on the two vessels had every sail deployed to go as quickly as possible while we were underway.

Our two vessels were well-equipped with instruments, compass, telescope, water depth measures, and the best reef sails, jib, and mainsail so that, with a good wind behind us to help keep us on our course with a lot of speed, within an hour we were in full sight of the vessel by telescope, and we discovered that it was Spanish, identified as a naval vessel named the Corvette *Atrevida*, a war sloop loaded with armed men on the decks and evidently well-manned with seafarers quite aware of the difficulties and dangers of commerce.

As we drew near, we saluted the glorious sight with a cannon shot as we intercepted the vessel at about 88 degrees, 14 minutes west longitude and 22 degrees, 12 minutes north latitude, as best I remember. General violence erupted aboard the Spanish ship, and we could scarcely believe that a mutiny was occurring so quickly. But the cries convinced us, for there were quarrels among the men, and several minutes later we could see them throwing men into the water. We could see that a few mutineers had succeeded in locking their officers in the forecastle before more than five of their adversaries could get up from below.

The few officers who were separated and kept below far from the officers locked in the forecastle were sweet-talking the mutineers, doubtlessly hoping they could persuade the other men below to give themselves up. The result was that those below without any weapons had to surrender to the officers after a short struggle, causing them to lose their capability of continuing the mutiny.

A scene of the most terrible carnage followed after the officers were freed. They ordered that the mutineers be bound and forced to go up on deck, where the officers ordered the chef, the black cook, to hit each one on the head with an axe and, afterwards, throw them into the sea.

Since my brother and I had learned how our ancestors had been persecuted and locked up in dungeons, tortured to death, and others exiled forever, it was terrible to be a witness to this act of diabolical barbarism on the vessel, but as incredible as it may appear, Spanish officers have always perpetrated the same cruelties. Pierre and I were witnesses to the second human torture and executions in June 1801.

Our vessel then continued slowly, and Uncle Reyné's vessel was almost at starboard to the right of the Spanish vessel; Pierre and I with our vessel were at starboard to the left. Their decks swarmed with men who were trying to hide so as not to be seen by our vessels, which were already in close and within firing range. No one could be seen on the decks of the Spanish vessel when we closed to about 60 meters distance, but we could see 15 dead bodies stretched out on their second and lower decks.

As the language of our vessel was French, the conversations between us doubtless were overheard by some of them who understood, so, when our vessel was just approaching, a man at the mizzen mast on the Spanish vessel gave a cry of joy in French: "*Vive la France!*" The words were scarcely out of his mouth when the Spanish vessel's lieutenant, being on the alert, shot him and he fell dead.

The captain of our vessel, Uncle Reyné, was almost to the starboard of the Spanish vessel, and being very upset by the brutal massacre of the Frenchman, began action by using his megaphone to demand a total surrender by the Spanish officers and commanding them to order their armed men to come up on deck and lower their sails.

There was no response after a moment's wait, and we did not have any more time to ask questions or for speculation since we saw them, in advance, arranging the springs on their cables to get ready to put their vessel to starboard in order to descend upon us so they could be in firing position, for they thought that our intentions were to run low and board their vessel with our small boats.

But such an effort to take advantage of the opportunity prepared by them (for they anticipated our men would follow) to fire upon us with a volley of small arms fire when our vessels were close by could have been a disaster, and they would have been able to win by maneuvering enough to at least stop our advance.

There was no answer even after the second moment had gone by. Consequently, Captain Reyné began to send signals to our vessel to prepare for the capture and gave the order to his cannon-eers to fire a direct twelve-pound shot at the bowsprit of the Span-ish vessel.

The Spanish captain, after hearing the volley and the ruin of his bowsprit, ordered all his men to get out and better prepare themselves to confront us, since he thought that we were prepar-ing ourselves for an attack.

All our men were fully ready and at their positions when Uncle Reyné gave the signal to Pierre and me to command our first and second cannoneers to fire the twelve-pound and twenty-pound cannons twice. We agreed that no opportunity could have been more favorable to us at that moment for the execution of our plans. Our shots produced the most terrible effect: the double discharges of our two cannons tore into and through the lower deck and cut their mizzen sail and also shattered their foretop at the top of their foremast, killing two of their officers and ten men on the spot and throwing at least eight men into the water.

The others, so frightened that they completely lost their heads, began to retreat like wild men in all directions on the decks, cry-ing and shouting with expressions of horror at the thought of be-ing forced to surrender. The destruction around them surpassed their greatest expectation of seeing themselves surrounded in des-perate condition, their discipline completely broken into an abso-lute incapability of defending themselves. But those Spanish offic-ers had truly harvested the perfect and complete fruits of the be-trayal of their crew; we did not give them enough time to recover from their panic and confusion as they jumped from deck to deck to prepare themselves for the rafts or jumped overboard into the sea.

Uncle Reyné's signal for our new attack ordered us to launch the assault, with orders to all our men immediately to take control of the entrances of the gangway and to attempt to open up a pas-sage on board for us. However, it soon became evident that this action would cost us very dearly despite the fact that the entire crew of the Spanish vessel was in a state of total confusion.

Uncle Reyné realized that the Spanish crew members who had stayed hidden between decks and in the holds were all armed and in perfect physical condition. After a short conversation between Uncle Reyné and his chief cannoneers with the purpose of finding a way to board the Spanish vessel without it costing us too many losses, we benefitted from the effects of a strong breeze which suddenly blew in such a way that the sterns of our vessels touched, which put us in a better position to throw our lines onto their capstans and tie up to their bowsprit so that our men could jump on board more easily and take control of the vessel. We took over the main deck without much difficulty, and immediately we took up position behind the spars that had been broken by our first cannon fire.

As soon as we held a secure position, and taking great care to avoid the risk of fire from the Spaniards who were still hidden below the decks, we decided that the first thing to do was to command the Spanish officers to be the first to come out from their hiding places. The Spanish officers surrendered, and we immediately made them line up behind the broken bowsprit of their vessel so that we could search and disarm them.

When that was done, we gave them orders to command their petty officers and men to obey and surrender: The Spanish officers and their lieutenants obeyed and commanded their men to be prisoners. We were very surprised to see the Spanish captain hold out his wrists so that we could put manacles on him; next, we fastened the soldiers two by two with manacles to a chain that ran between them; then we put them in the cells of the prisons located on board our vessels.

It was soon evident that this was the first time they had seen a privateer crew. Our first concern afterward was to find a good place for the imprisonment and treatment of their wounded, as well as finding a different area in our prison to put the hard headed ones who were still hidden in the vessel.

We chose one of the captured lieutenants and the men he had under his command to guide five of our armed men into the holds of the captured vessel to find those who were still hidden. Our men had to climb barrels piled almost to the ceiling; they also had a lot of difficulty in opening a passage in the lower hold, half filled with corn that was very well reinforced with planks. We found some men who still had pistols in their belts, as well as a certain number of muskets with bayonets. We ordered them to surrender and go up on deck to be searched.

When we had disarmed all the men of the Spanish warship *Atrevida*, we congratulated ourselves on the security of our situation. Next, we took the names and called the roll of all our prisoners so as to classify them according to their worth. Some had to submit to a strict regimen while others were hired for wages, which pleased them infinitely more than what they received from their superiors while they were under the yoke of the Spanish crown.

All the weapons and munitions that were on the Spanish vessel were now in our possession; the officers were under lock and key, and the future of our prisoners was no longer uncertain.

We began to make a general search of the vessel because we knew that there were gold and silver articles in the holds of the vessel. Before making a short list for the search, we decided to free the captain from our vessel's prison to go with us on the search for the gold and silver hidden somewhere in the holds of his vessel. No persuasion could prevail upon him to reveal the exact locations of the gold and silver until, finally, we had to drag him on the deck to meditate in the heat of the full sun.

Our first reason for grilling the captain was that he had hidden the vessel's logs; the second reason was that it was quite possible that there were men hidden all over, ready to fire on us; the third reason was that we had to work very quickly because the vessels were drifting, and even then they had drifted far from the spot where we had intercepted and captured the vessel as a prize.

After about 45 minutes, the captain was exhausted with the effect of the sun's heat and, in fact, so weak that he could scarcely get up or speak. Yet he continued to refuse to confess and reveal the exact location of the hidden treasure; Uncle Reyné suggested that we had to try to force a confession by using a magnifying glass to focus more of the sun's heat on him and, at the same time, firing our pistols close to his ears to create a vibration of his nerves combined with the increased heat of the sun. The subsequent events proved that the noise of the pistols with the applied heat prodded his senses and mind to repent and reveal the location of the gold and silver materials and his own iron chests.

Uncle Reyné and his first lieutenant decided to discuss the matter with our two crews in order to gather round the feeble creature and reprimand him morally to make him meditate and ponder his other acts of inhuman torture and the lives that he had caused to be taken in the past, to torment his conscience over the mutineers he had killed and thrown into the sea the day before, and his entire past, in which he had gladly acquiesced, under the orders of the viceroys of Spain, Mexico, and the island of Cuba, to persecute all Frenchmen.

When Uncle Reyné had rebuked the Spanish captain to a moral degree of conscience, not considering him even by profession, worthy of execution for his guilt in the deaths of those whom we had seen in mutiny the day before we captured his warship, Uncle Reyné passed judgment on him, to spare his life by separating him from the Spanish sovereigns and viceroys and having him sequestered in a French colony at forced labor for life.

Uncle Reyné always advised Pierre and me, as much as possible, to use a system of sparing the lives of Spanish officers so they might pass before their prisoners (when they are liberated from the Spanish yoke) to see them spit in their faces as examples of what changes can happen to people with orthodox minds and a cowardly past and then exile them for life in the French colonies as object lessons in different territories.

I write my words as the truth on the subject of the past of the Spaniards. At this moment Spain is known among its various possessions as the cruelest nation and will be exposed and known much more in the future, along with another brute, which is to say: England.

I am not a poet who writes simply for just any curious person, nor even to satisfy my own curiosity. I feel that I must compile records that are almost too old to hold together and are ready to fall into ruin: a chronicle to compile for my grandchildren that they alone may keep and no one else will know of, but I have suffered under the abuses of Spain at war with France. I lost many relatives on my mother's side who suffered because of the Inquisitions against the Jews and also an Inquisition against the French in the Spanish provinces.

I had an uncle who was 20 years younger than my father, who had suffered under the Mexican viceroys. My Uncle Jean was separated from the relatives of his mother and imprisoned in the dirty dungeons of Mexico City for more than two years, his property confiscated. After that, he left for an unknown location when he was about 20. My Uncle Jean was of the same nationality as the family from which I descended.

I remember having seen him only one time; I was about four years old when my uncle, aged 16, left on a ship with his relatives from Cadiz to visit our family house at Port-au-Prince. My uncle came with his Uncle Bernard Miramon and the family of Marcus La Porta, who were relatives of his mother. They stayed with us for a week, more or less, and then they left for Vera Cruz. I never saw him after that, but when I was about 14 I received the news that he had been exiled to some part of Cuba to go to die.

Marcus La Porta escaped and came to our house when I was 15, telling us stories about the flight of the French from the provinces of Mexico and South America. I had a cousin named Alexandre Manuel Laffite, who also suffered in the northern provinces of South America.

Uncle Reyné suggested that we free two of the subordinate officers of the Spanish captain from the brig of our vessel to accompany us, with him in the lead, to go through the lower holds to show us the exact locations of the hidden material that we were interested in looking for. After our complete search of the secret parts of the vessel was completed, we then began to make a short audit of the accounts—or an inventory of the secret logs, that we found and kept, about the loading of the Spanish vessel at Vera Cruz for the trip east to Cuba and Spain. These ship logs helped us a great deal later on; they were a disguised stroke of luck for our privateers who sailed forth to capture Spanish vessels.

Our complete inventory of the captured Spanish prize consisted of a warship with 73 men; 42 of those men were navy sailors. We verified and found that 47 men were missing from the crew of 120 men that the *Atrevida* had while leaving Vera Cruz before the mutiny and our seizure of the vessel. The *Atrevida* had eight nine-kilogram cannons, ten light cannons called carronades, twelve pivot cannons called *canons d'espingle* and waterproof weapons chests. It was a 400-ton vessel built as a combination naval and commercial vessel. It had many oceanographic charts piled up in the observation cabin, which became information of great value to us for subsequent privateering ventures.

The total value of the merchandise consisted of 20 [sic] kilograms of grain (cereal); 120 bales of maguey fiber, which on average weighed 60 kilograms each; tanned horse and cow hides; gold, silver, and bronze artilcles; iron strongboxes that held gold doubloons—hidden in the barrels of cereal (or corn).

After we made the complete inventory, we began to have the treasures and the gold and silver transported to our vessels, as they were still attached to the Spanish vessels, so that they would be fairly easy to transport; and we left the majority of the other merchandise on the vessel since there was no need of steering until the winds became more favorable, either from the north or from the west.

Our two vessels were well-equipped and furnished with extra canvas sailcloth for unforeseen events before we left the port of our city, Port-au-Prince. Consequently, there was no problem in putting the captured Spaniards to work at rigging new sails in the place of their sails that we had ripped up during the capture.

All three vessels were fastened together until the repair and transport of all the valuables had ended. From the time of the seizure up to that time, we discovered that the vessels had drifted about 50 kilometers southeast with the sea currents almost to Point Catoche on the northern coast of the Yucatan on the following day, April 23.

On that day the wind picked up to 21 kilometers, which gave us the chance to set our sails for the southeast, close to Pedro at longitude 99 degrees, 15 minutes west, latitude 17 degrees, 12 minutes north while no wind would come at us from the front because we were going east toward the first French market, the port of Fort-de-France, Martinique.

Captain Reyné's vessel was 300 tons, well-constructed, well-armed and equipped with 15 carronades that fired shot that weighed six kilograms, eight very long cannons that fired shot of ten kilograms avoirdupois [sic], ten blunderbusses and waterproof strong-boxes for each of them, and a well-disciplined crew of 60 hardy men.

On our vessel of 300 tons, Pierre and I had a crew of 50 robust, well- disciplined men; our vessel was of good construction, light and well-equipped with ten naval cannons that fired six kilogram avoirdupois balls, six cannons that fired ten kilogram shot, eight brass blunderbusses, and strongboxes for each.

Uncle Reyné assigned Pierre the helm of the Spanish vessel, and I was to command the second vessel. Uncle Reyné led with his vessel; consequently, all the vessels were ready to sail a parallel to the east without difficulty.

We regaled all the prisoners with the best meats and wines; they felt perfectly happy——with the exception of a few Spanish officers who felt fear and terror concerning their destiny in the French colonies under the military officers of France and being used against their very own nation, Spain.

They did not yet know or realize that the sovereigns under the crown of Spain were very afraid on account of the triumph of the great French Revolution. The Spanish officers were from the upper classes of society and, naturally, were hypocrites with disguised personalities, but they were so degenerate that they neither could nor would understand the lower masses, the common people of their nation and their American provinces held under an iron hand, with the result that those officers were accustomed to consider their kind of government as something sacred and unchangeable, like the Church or a sky in Spain itself.

From the point of view of progress, Spain——that despotic nation which once was great——attained its own condemnation of decadence governed by dull-witted monarchs with blood diseases in their veins, who pursued an Inquisition against the Jews for 300 years and another against the French in Mexico and all South America during the French Revolution and who made unjust, despotic laws in their own nation simply to grant feudal privileges to a series of patriarchs who had only time to be swept away with everything they considered just and holy in Spain and because of the fear that their American colonial system was threatened with destruction.

The Spanish bureaucrats had such an orthodox mentality, with their church commingled with their pagan government like one body, that they could or would not consider accepting Latin America at all. The panic-stricken Spanish bureaucrats thought they saw spies and agitators everywhere coming out of the French Revolution into the Spanish domains, which caused all Frenchmen to be looked upon as dangerous and impious.

The viceroys in Mexico only found solace through their system of persecuting everything that was French. The French were imprisoned, their property seized, some reduced to slavery; and many were deported under the pretext that they were impious for not having regularly complied with the formality of attending mass in a church. Pedro Valenzuela was the brute who had been the chief agent under the viceroy in Mexico entrusted with the Inquisition against all the French, including some of my own relatives. The youngest brother of my father, Jean Laffite y Miramon, fell as its victim.

After our complete interrogation of each of the men of the captured *Atrevida*, we found that nine men were French prisoners, forced to work their passage as slaves for their deportation out of Mexico. Their unusual behavior as we traveled to Martinique finally caught our attention, and we freed them immediately and took them into our employ as equals to help us transport our prizes to Fort-de-France,

We continued to sail on a course to the east with our captured prize under variable weather for eight days without incident, except for encountering a light cool wind at 71 degrees , 14 minutes west longitude and 16 degrees, 21 minutes north, until we arrived in full view of Fort-de-France. A cannon salvo burst above the harbor to greet our vessels as soon as we were recognized and identified by our waving privateer banners. As a matter of curiosity we were very happy and amused to see what would happen later. The seventh day, after our sales were completed, we were very happy with big money orders and good letters of credit that awaited us in Paris.

Peace between France and England was ending, and the flames of war broke out again until Mr. Bonaparte quenched the flames in 1803 by bringing all continental Europe to his feet. During that time Uncle Reyné very rapidly became a man of importance, and there were rumors that he was a man honorably engaged in heroic efforts in the seizure of captured prizes of great value, which he contributed to Mr. Bonaparte for the defense and preservation of French freedom.

After all our sales and inventories were ended at Fort-de-France, we then went to Port-au-Prince, carrying with us doubloons and a few prisoners of the captured *Atrevida* in order to modify and renovate it into a different type of vessel.

Our grandmother, Pierre's wife, and mine were the first to embrace us upon our arrival in the harbor of Port-Au-Prince. Our Uncle Reyné, our grandmother, and our father sat down together to talk about our long absence. Our father was always a joyful listener, and he was calm like our brothers Marcus and Henri, who had a penchant toward pessimism and did not have much interest in the business of privateers because their own was a leather shop and had nothing to do with the sea.

Our city of Port-au-Prince began to sense and undergo a change caused by Toussaint l'Ouverture's leading the Negro slaves with a certain fury against the lighter colored Negroes, who were a free people and possessed slaves. Toussaint l'Ouverture and Henri Christophe were two educated Negroes who directed and fomented the insurrection for absolute independence of black Negroes in the western part of Santo Domingo, choosing an Indian name, *"Haïti,"* which is now considered a republic. The two Negro leaders had an excellent education and, doubtless, had a full right to freedom and independence because France was stifled on every side by the British danger and the despotic crown of Spain.

Mr. Bonaparte thought that the slaves of Santo Domingo had the right to establish a little, autonomous republic, but he strongly resented that a nation, no matter which, would smuggle munitions and firearms into the hands of illiterates in an attempt at an insurrection for independence.

At the end of October our Uncle Reyné was highly praised and invited to dine with Mr. Bonaparte, and he accepted a very high rank in the military service of France, just like our brother Alexandre, who was already in the French military as an expert cannoneer. Pierre and I began to miss our brother Alexandre and we would miss our Uncle Reyné very much after he enlisted as a technician in the artillery of Bonaparte. We thus felt that, sooner or later, it would be our sacred duty to enter France's military service. Our grandmother and our wives discouraged Pierre and me from going to France to join the military so soon.

Before he left for France, Uncle Reyné advised Pierre and me by suggesting that we had a marvelous opportunity to go enlist under letters of marque as privateers against Spanish and British shipping as a good deed and as a benefit for the country of France. Pierre and I obtained letters of marque to sail the open sea to capture enemy vessels and their cargo in the same way as I already mentioned in detail concerning the naval battle of the corvette *Atrevida* captured in April 1801.

First, we organized a few men into a secret general staff to use as spies to send us information about the departures of British and Spanish vessels.

Jean Laffite

LOUISIANA

Toledo: Saturday, November 8, 1845

Put yourself at a distance; afterward, approach yourself and meet yourself, and you will know how to master yourself.

We took the ship for France in September 1801. In October 1801 we embarked for London. Arrested with Pierre in London, we served a 50-day sentence for vagrancy, but we took ship at London for Bilbao, Spain, in January 1802. We were arrested for expressing our opinions in regard to Santo Domingo; we served 30 days without food during our imprisonment, except what we could beg.

We worked in a rope factory after being freed in Bilbao, and in March 1802, we walked about 120 kilometers to Orduña until May 1802. We walked on roads through the mountains to Irun, Biarritz, then to Gascony. We spent a few days at Dax then we went through the mountains [sic] to Bayonne. In June 1802 we met our Uncle Reyné at Arcachon and stayed there for two weeks. Uncle Reyné was a cannoneer in the French army.

In July 1802 we walked to Bordeaux; then we embarked for Port-au-Prince in August 1802. Enlisted to serve in the colonial army as cannoneers for one year in Port-au-Prince, we were duped by Spanish officers in Santo Domingo. Smuggling between Spain and the slaves in Port-au-Prince began during those dark years. Our service was also on board vessels with the mission of seeking out Spanish vessels and seizing flints and gunpowder.

Our brother Alexandre was to enlist as a privateer, too. Uncle Reyné and Alexandre were distinguished, decorated cannoneers during their military service. Our hatred for Spain and England became stronger.

Pierre and I had visited New Orleans for the first time in 1799 with our Uncle Felix and two brothers-in-law, Jean La Porte and Eugène La Porte. I was then 17. When Louisiana was taken by the French from the Spanish, consequently, for almost six weeks during November and December 1803, Louisiana was French.

Our brother Alexandre received serious powder burns on his left eye.

Pierre and I could divide our time equally between Port-au-Prince and New Orleans, and we were happy beyond our greatest hopes. Toward the end of 1803 we discovered that four British frigates were sent secretly to leave for Vera Cruz under orders to withdraw the public treasury of Mexico: two millions of gold and silver coins. Pierre and I had two well equipped vessels with materiel and the best cannoneers to capture any vessel easily. Two of those vessels were captured, consisting of a small quantity of merchandise that the British used to cover bars of gold and silver goods.

In October 1804 our brother Alexandre, Pierre, and I requested a privateering commission against the English and Spanish vessels. In November 1804 we embarked for Cuba to capture our seventeenth vessel loaded with slaves. We embarked for Mobile to sell the slaves, a very weak market, and many customs duties. We embarked for New Orleans, likewise with very little luck with the slaves there. We again set out to sea, trying to find bases for unloading. We found Grande Terre and Grande Isle, and we gave the slaves to a fisherman.

We returned to Port-au-Prince to help all the refugees disembark along the lower Mississippi River. Returning to Port-au-Prince in January 1805, we were encountered by some Spanish vessels and were taken away as prisoners, losing all our property and money.

In March 1805 we engaged in an audacious and reckless combat, capturing seven vessels with a single little sloop that we had captured after being freed in Cuba. We embarked for Grand Terre to help the little fishing boats.

What you judge good for another, first try yourself. Man is not governed by the voice of his conscience but by the voices of those around

*him. Watch out for malcontents; if they acquire great wealth, they be-
come rapacious dangers to liberty.*

Messrs. Perrin, Rigaud, and Chighizola helped us draw maps
of the commercial bases along the marshy waterways of south Louisiana. Our first base was Grande Terre and the second Barataria.
Our brother Alexandre, Pierre, and I had registered our vessels in
New Orleans, which gave us a good reception point for our operations.

Mr. Herman Grammaton was enlisted as an officer, Mr. Louis
Chighizola, and Mr. François Rigaud were enlisted as strongbox
guards and policemen. Mr. Vincent Gambai also enlisted with the
rank of captain as a master cannoneer, Mr. Robert Johnston and
Mr. Jean Desfarges as master cannoneers and navigators.

By establishing our commune on the island of Grande Terre
and our warehouses along the bay of Louisiana and in New Orleans with a well paid and disciplined secret police service, we
created the need for new markets; we constructed a blacksmith
shop in 1805 in New Orleans. We held our first meeting at Grande
Terre in October, November, and December 1805 for the officers
in a secret conference concerning the police guard.

Pierre was sick during the summer of 1805; in the summer of
1806 he was sick for the second time because of the heat and
drink. For sometime he was an American official in New Orleans,
but when his generosity was taken advantage of by newcomers, he
resigned. From that moment on our reputation as smugglers was
more assured than ever.

All the territorial officials bought or accepted smuggled goods.
At first Mr. Claiborne somewhat approved the sale of our goods,
but then he began to raise a protest when our commune grew and
fortified itself. Our commune organized the smugglers in independent groups, looking out for one another. Before our arrival,
smuggling by fishermen, smugglers of little skill, had been stopped.
Mr. Claiborne and I met in New Orleans to discuss the subject of
my merchandise on his birthday in 1805. I gave him some silk
goods and some good quality cloth that he accepted without too

much protest. The transactions were done behind closed doors and for five years we were unknown by distant buyers.

I had three vessels authorized without any questions by the French consul in New Orleans. I gave Bordeaux as my birth place in 1780.

Towards 1808 Mr. Grymes and Mr. Claiborne opposed our expansion; for a while Mr. Grymes calmed Mr. Claiborne. Because of his difficult position, the latter persisted and attempted to do away with our expansion.

We built a store in July 1807 in New Orleans; we constructed a depot in March 1808 in Donaldsonville. We built a provisions storehouse, Petit Temple, in the west of San Salvador in February 1810. We built a warehouse in Barataria in January 1808. We built a sale house, Grand Temple, in October 1811. We built a warehouse for powder and flints in San Salvador in December 1812.

In 1812 Mr. Claiborne declared himself openly, but that publicity attracted new buyers. Other warehouses were opened in a radius of 150 miles of New Orleans. My requests for personal meetings with Mr. Claiborne were rejected. Mr. Grymes resigned; the members of the legislature were in favor of our commune; Mr. Claiborne exceeded his authority by promulgating laws harmful to the interests of the native Creoles.

I then made laws opposed to Mr. Claiborne's. My letters of patent obtained from different sources legitimized my vessels' attacks against the aggression of enemy nations, principally Spain and England. My only guilt was from running contraband against the customs regulations of the United States. The original reasons that pushed me into smuggling were the conduct of several American customs officers who with excessive zeal played the role of proprietors by demanding sums much higher than the regular duties to satisfy their personal interests. My brother Pierre, who was an American official, was witness to some of their dishonest dealings, which victimized the native Creoles of New Orleans. He resigned rather than participate in their depredations upon the good Frenchmen of Louisiana.

After the Americans' purchase of Louisiana, a contrast was established in New Orleans, on one side the French, strictly loyal to their faith and hardworking, and on the other side individuals of English origin, without faith or law. I kept up my generous actions toward the good people, coming to their aid with all the necessities of their lives, both material and spiritual.

I asked the opinion of several advisors so that they might help me find a way of getting my goods through without using cheats as middlemen. Everywhere there was a demand for workers and merchandise to be able to make progress.

Mr. Claiborne had posted the promise of a reward of 500 dollars for my arrest on the fourth Monday of November, 1813. I had a reward of 1500 dollars posted for the arrest of Mr. Claiborne on the last Saturday of November 1813. I gave secret instructions to my officers to confiscate the merchandise which was at his house, and I promised to pay three times the value of those goods, 15,000 dollars, to my officers in Barataria. I had a sword offered to Mr. Claiborne to fight a duel: "If he refuses, slap him, and force him to resign when he leaves the prison of Grande Terre."

This publicity increased the number of markets. In those troubled times I always gave proof of generosity toward the worthy, good people of New Orleans and the vicinity.

I requested more commissions from the fortress of Cartagena. Disputes arose among the Italians of our commune. Mr. Brown, whose real name was Benito Ratti, Mr. Chighizola, and Mr. Gambai did not want to join us. They did so later. Mr. Gambai went off to do his own smuggling. My vessel, the *Dorada,* received its letters of patent from Cartagena in 1809. I gave my vessel *Philanthrope* to Mr. Gambai in 1810, and the preceding year I had given the *Tigre* to my brother Alexandre.

I have never claimed to be anything other than a wandering liberator of the suffering throngs, only to undergo periods of exile, imprisonment, poverty, condemnations, and suffering caused by the despotic laws of men. I was young, handsome, generous, honest, ambitious, and not responsible for acts committed by others who were responsible. I owe all my ingenuity to the great intuition of my Spanish Jewish grandmother, who had been a witness to the era of the Inquisition.

At 22 I fought a duel with an English officer on board his vessel the *Fox*. My second duel took place when I was still 22 with a Spanish Mulatto officer on his ship *Aires de Mora*. On those two ships everyone was a prisoner sent into exile. I questioned them to ascertain their skills and recruited them as crew for my vessels, and they became privateers fighting against England and Spain.

We scattered 102 English prisoners along the coastal regions from Mobile to Campeche, some others a few years later in Barataria.

The founders of good will and inventors of methods of progress never signed their names. My brother Alexandre changed his name, then took a nickname. I would have done the same under different circumstances.

Never tell the same story several times, for only those of slight intelligence blow their own horns.

I have lived and traveled with little and have felt happy.

Latin American favored privateering vessels to operate against all Spanish vessels and shipping. For periods of six months, one year, and two years eminent officers served on my general staff on land and on vessels. For the progress and well being of the communes, others were assigned to duties of liaison between land and sea in accordance with their qualifications and the necessary conditions but not according to their needs or desires: I shall give their names, those of my staff on land and sea, and the names of my vessels that I commanded from the age of 19.

Spain and England were the principal authors of laws against privateers. From 1818 until 1824, Russia, the United States, England, and Spain enforced under treaty the laws to ally themselves militarily on the high seas to eliminate the privateer vessels that operated against shipping.

My officers were artillery commanders, astronomers, chief navigators, secret service agents, messengers, chief accountants, office clerk-salesmen, chief blacksmiths, master carpenters, doctors, cannon powder makers, policemen, subordinates.

Brother Alexandre known as Dominque Youx, brother Pierre, Uncle Reyné Beluchai, Felix Beluchai, Antoine Beluchai, and cousins Jean de LaPorte, Eugène de LaPorte, Jérôme de LaPorte, Manuel Perrin, Edouard de LaPorte.

Captains: Antoine Dubois, Js Campbell, André Grannette, Arsène Lebleu, James Brown, Jules Cartier, Jn Marotte, Paul Gounod, José Iuana, Vincent Rensand, Robert Johnson, Renné Joffre, Alexandre Daguerre, Jn Farrel, Calvin Hillman, José Martino, Jn Amigone, Hernan Ortiz, Rafel de Lisa, Daldir Berret, Pierre Ampère, Troyan Gravier, Antoine Corbière, Barthélémy Lafon, François Boysnet, Irygoyen Berretera, François Tomas, Pierre Liguet, Jn Desfarges, Pierre Sicard, Amon Clozelle, Jn Champlain, William Mitchell, Claude Forain, Manuel Lopez, Vincent Gambai, Jn Betancourt, Reyle Lacassier, Antonio Angelo, Pierre Gual, Jn Celard, Manuel Moreno, Jn Constant, Jn Guérin, Jn Juanillo, Auguste Commines, Antoine Piromeace, Tomas Cos, Samuel Huette, Js Black, Laurent Maire, Polito Medina, Euthelère Maire, Henri Marguère, Louis Durieux, Antoine Baudelaire, Jn Hamette, Jn Marsaleri, Lucia Pérez, Js Clark, Jn Gallardo, José Clemente, Louis Iturribarria, Gustave Duval, Jn de Gutierrez.

Attorneys: Edouard Livingston, Jn Grymes, Pierre Morel, José Broutin.

Advisors: Pierre Clément Laussat, Narcisse Broutin, Jn Blanque, Samuel Williams, Bernard Marigny, José Roffignac, Louis Louaillier, Auguste Davezac.

Policemen: François Rigaud, Louis Chighizola, Manuel Perrin, Jn Ducoing, Antoine Durieux, Jn Pereneau, Js de la Borde, Pierre Cadet, Jn Little, Gerald Mortimore, Theodore Rawlins, Aurelio Fuentes, Henri Geme, Manuel Bazo, Martin Pouse, Pierre Terrain, Jule Thracuis, Charles Lominne, Jn Gentille, Eugène Renard.

Master Carpenters: Jn Perez, Jesse Pina, Jn Currier, Antoine Bronte, Jn M. Converse.

Chief Blacksmiths: André Thiacus, Ignace Thiacus.

Continuation: the following:

Chief navigators, astronomers, artillery commanders, chief accountants, office clerk-salemen, secret agents, doctors, messengers, powder makers, and subordinates.

John B. Laporte, Pierre La Maison, Daniel Smith, Ross Chapman, Henri Peire, Jn Roldofo, Herman Grammaton, François Dupuis, Jn B.C. Rousselin, André Rieux, Henri Perry, Vincent Dupare, Jacques Cannon, Jean A Humbert, André Whitman, Jn M. Picornelli, Jn West, Alexandre St Elmo, Seren Courtais, Jn Dutrieux, José De Toledo, Louis De Arury, Benito De Ariza, Jn Leal de Franca, David De Forrest, Louis Brion, Raymond Espagnol, José de Place, Benj. Laveau, Claude Hudspeth, Jn B. Arnaud, André Rieux, Joachim Sautas, Renné Roland, Dennis Thomas, José A. Martina, Arsène L. Latour, Antoine Laverge, Alexandre Barrival, Pierre Rosselin, José De Huerrera [sic], François De Rieux, Abner Duncan, André Renaud, Eugène De Thomas, Eugène de Jammes, Jn Faquare, Jn Guerre de Ruida, Jn McHenry, Ernst Bramlit, William Cochrane, Louis Noël, Jn Trickert, Jn Hervien, Jn Sauvinet, Nunzio Granato, Pierre Gilotte, Etienne Evan Jones, André Robin, Antoine L. Lallemand, Jn Mayier, Antoine Sennette, Jn Reynier, Antoine Angelette, José Valliert, Jn B. Soulize, Juan Lopez, Ch. Dickinson, Alcida Gervin Conchol, Henri Seybasdier, Jn McGhee, Henri Chez Seymour, Jn Irenne Devereaux, Jules Beratte, Antoine de Savarier, Jn Davez, Edouard Marcelin, Louis Louaililler [sic], Angel Raballo, Bernard Mandeville, Constant Le Clerq, Antoine Cordier, Salvator Artique, Antoine Bormette, William McClure, Jn. Antoine Ranchier, Louis Dalhier, Ellis Polk Beanne, Jules Sedonier, Louis P. Chenier, Louis Philippe, Issac Tilette, Jn. Kluson, André Como Coppée, Manuel Guerra García, Antoine M. De Monatague, Tryon Thompson, Laurent Pages Ponsard, Octave Fénelon, André Abelard, Jn Stelsas, Henri Corne Nuñez, Michel J. Joffre, Jn Cousins, Ephraim Thompkins, Raymond Ranchier, Alexandre la Bruyère, Jacques Bornier, Js Bowie, Henry Bentely, Jn Bowie, François Chevraud, Evan Epps.

Jean Laffite

Saint Louis, Monday, January 12, 1846

The names of my vessels were *Jupiter, Dulcinée, Ancuda, El Tigre, Ambrosia, Eloise, Aberdaine, Espina, Almirante, Eleanor, Amiable María, Extase, Beltramy, Flora Américain, Arismendi, Golfe de Madame, Belmonte, Guèpe, Blanque-rez, Genny, Bisboa, Galant Homme, Belgarde, Brave, Huntress, Bolívar, Hotspur, Belona, Hector, Bâtiment-Prix, Hermanos Dos, Congrès, Imprimer, Cassadore, Cometa, Ilusoire, Carmelita, Imprenable, Chauvina, Iturribe, Columbo, Luton, Concord, Ciel-Bleu, Intrépide, Confiant, Louisa Antoine, Corona, Lune de Novembre, Devador, Lion Marin, Dorada, Misère, Diligent, Melita, Montería, Felicita, Le Espion, Jameson, La Soeur Chérie, Le Pandoure, Industria, Ninfa, Nancy, Nonagon, Insociaux, Franklin, Sapris, Sinega, Saturnía, Séraphique, Victoria, Success, Caria, Tonnère, Petit Milan, Philanthrope, Orquel, Petronilla, Penrith, Pomora, Placton, Raqueur, Rita, Feaux Feluca, Saragosa, San Antonio, Strabania, Salir Salix, Sinue Que Non, Espionne, Wilgas, Véloce, Singerie Nargues, Républican, Actina, Renard, Antonio Bonafacia.*

My vessels won in every battle on the coasts of Louisiana, in the south of the Gulf, on the high seas, and all throughout the great islands of the Indies, the little Virgin Islands, and the northern coasts of South America. They brought back many vessels to be repaired and given new names. Some damaged Spanish or English vessels were left in the middle of the ocean to be burned.

The colonial states underwent a blockade and could ship out nothing on the high seas. The city of Washington fell into the hands of the English. The cities and the ports on the Atlantic were blockaded. All held out well and peerlessly despite the British pressure on America.

Pierre and I requested a commission as privateers against the English and Spanish vessels in 1813 in New Orleans. My brother Alexandre also asked for a privateering commission under any available flag against the English and Spanish vessels in 1812: Captain Alexandre, A.K.A. Dominque Youx of the privateer named the *Pandoure*, September 1812, New Orleans.

My vessels were engaged in several battles on the high seas against English and Spanish war vessels. The United States was suffering setbacks and losses. I was sending messages about the English invaders coming on the high sea; my messengers never returned from The city of Washington. I decided to send messengers with a second warning to General Winder; they never came back. My warning messages to Washington were ignored or doubtless never reached the officials to whom they were destined; my messengers never returned.

The officers of the crews of the English vessels continued to communicate with me for eight months, insisting I release their vessels and free their prisoners. I handed over some of their vessels to Latin America, and I scattered the British prisoners along the coasts of Mexico and South America.

Having no news from my messengers to the city of Washington, the British pressure was what the American officials were aware of. I subsequently sent new warnings to the officials of New Orleans, but they in their turn ignored me. I received many insults from the officials of New Orleans, and later from the city of Washington, I received insults and threats.

It is as criminal to tell lies and to hoard as wine is a good nourishment.

I sent messages up the Mississippi; few cities along the Mississippi were warned by other good Americans. My messages were accepted and supported by a large number of Frenchmen near Saint Louis. One of the inhabitants of that city thought ahead and employed good tactics to keep the Indian tribes from joining up with English agents: those British agents were dangerous at the time. That Spanish inhabitant was a good, great man: Emanuel Lisa.

In the meantime, the English, believing that I was weak on the Gulf coast of Louisiana, tried to invade my territory. They ran into my expert cannoneers and were repulsed with heavy losses. The English then made new offers to my commune and me. The first offers were quite small and consisted of recognizing my right of government of their colonial possessions of the little islands south of Santo Domingo. Their second offers were better: making me the offer to accept an official position in their various possessions.

Their third offer reached the sum of 30,000 pounds British sterling. That would have been enough to tempt many Americans to sell out their land but not enough to understand that the greatest and most sacred manuscripts ever composed and written by men would have been erased from the face the earth, the great Declaration of Independence and the great Constitution of the United States.

However seductive those offers, they remained somnolent, and I did not pay any attention to them. I knew for a certainty that the great documents would have been effaced from the earth by the act of allowing the passage of the British through my communes or by helping their passage through New Orleans and up the Mississippi River.

Having no news of my messages to New Orleans, I decided to send Raymond Ranchier with messages as a third warning to Governor Claiborne and Jn Blanque.

Jn Laffite

Saint Louis, Tuesday, February 10, 1846

A pure faith and a strong mind in a man is stronger than his fear and his doubts; they will give him the rope upon which to hang his life. Simple as it is, place your confidence in your own mind and live courageously, and hope to gain more in so doing.

Using the Indian chiefs in the entire north of the country by mobilizing their Indians as allies would certainly have pulled all the states toward the Atlantic.

Letters written by my hand were shown to American officials in New Orleans. They mocked the letters and spit additional insults on my messages, making even more threats against me and my commune. I took the insults with good faith and a great heart, only continuing to fortify my own communes against the invaders.

Thanks to the heroic French of New Orleans and it surroundings and their heroic efforts to help me keep up the pressure on certain officials who held government positions and make them understand and be aware of the approach of the dangers coming from the enemy and despite all the credible warnings, despite still more insults and the great threat of a large reward for my capture, which was posted in all the highly visible areas of New Orleans, I called my officers together with a member of the legislature present at the meeting.

It was unanimously decided that I was to post a reward three times greater for the arrest of the governor; that the said governor be arrested and brought to the prison of my commune and deported back to Virginia; that elections take place to elect a military government, the same as the understanding with the French nationals of New Orleans. Certain of the displayed and returned English letters have doubtless been destroyed: I showed some to the officials of Cartagena, and they are probably destroyed too.

Despite the reward for my arrest, my brother Alexandre held an auction sale on the steps of the governor's residence: not one soldier, not one official objected to it.

In the street the people followed this battle of rewards with passionate interest; the hardship of the British blockade was making itself felt. The French did not know which side to take; they did not like England and had no desire to see the new American customs invade their city.

To backtrack, Mr. Devezac, Mr. Thiacus, and I proceeded to sell slaves and traded slaves at the Maspero Bank on Wednesday, November 11, 1812. The following Sunday, November 15, 1812, an army captain claimed that he had attacked a group of smugglers, some of whom were arrested while the others fled.

It was reported to the governor that I was . . . one of those who had escaped. I was ordered to appear before the tribunal while I was in the city. I appeared there on Thursday, April 16, 1812, to respond to the accusation made by the captain. I paid a bail of 14,000 dollars and was to be brought to trial on April 30, 1812. But neither the statements of my officers, who had to give complete verification of all the merchandise, nor those of my men who were under arrest supported those of the captain. I therefore did not appear before the court, but I gave to all the magistrates, from the most obscure officials to the governor himself, permission to take that bail money and put it to charitable use to succor the poor of New Orleans. My request was ignored, and nobody ever profited or learned what became of it, and even to this day probably no one knows.

From that day numerous complaints were filed against my brother and me. I spent the next spring in New Orleans with my brother Pierre and his family. My elder brother Alexandre took charge of the smuggling. The authorities still wanted to know where the third brother was. Our reply: "But he is in France."

During the summer of 1813, the summonses proliferated. We avoided them because the majority of the members of our commune were gathering with the intent of defending against the British invasion.

The first combat between my commune and the English ships took place at Caillou Pass on Tuesday, March 18, 1813. The English withdrew with heavy losses. The forces of my commune fought another battle against disembarking British troops on Wednesday, June 23, 1813. The English suffered additional losses at the entrance of Bayou La Fourche.

My officers called me to the Grande Terre commune after the twin successes of my cannoneers on the Louisiana coast. We met to plan our defense and tactics to use against another English aggression. At that moment my hands were full. I had to face up to and fight simultaneously on two fronts: first the English, then the governor's malice; several of my men abandoned me to become independent privateers. I did not lose many members of the commune.

On Wednesday, August 18, 1813, we engaged in combat for the third time against English warships, this time between La Barbade and Ile Saint Jean; and after disabling one of the warships, we set it on fire. The other English ships withdrew with heavy losses; two ships loaded with Negroes were brought to Grande Terre; as to the English prisoners, taken to South America, they were never to return from there.

On Thursday, November 18, 1813, a fishing boat claiming to be American, arrived at Grande Terre. They asked me to arrange a truce together with the English emissary. I gave no precise date. They reappeared the following Thursday, November 25; an English warship anchored near Grande Terre. Carrying a signal of truce, the British envoy attempted to establish an agreement aimed at fortifying the passes of the Mississippi. I warned him of the presence on the neighboring bays of a large number of heavily armed Americans who counted a great number of allies among the Indians. The British vessel weighed anchor without any agreement being made.

Meanwhile, my court summonses accumulated in New Orleans. My crew was accused with piracy in regard to the capture of a Spanish ship, *Santa*, on Friday, February 19, 1813, and of the capture of the ship named *Luisa Antonio* on Saturday, May 1, 1813. On Monday, April 26, 1813, the owner of the ship, Antonio Arcasas, registered a complaint asking to regain possession of its cargo. For the governor it was the dreamed opportunity to incite still more scandal.

We were never pirates. In fact, my tribunal tried and convicted pirates: it even deported some of them to other lands. My commune always operated under the authority of letters of patent. Those letters were issued by countries in constant struggle with rival nations. England, France, Spain, Mexico, Cartagena, and all the other countries awarded privateering licenses, considered as a legitimate business.

On Wednesday, November 24, 1813, the governor posted a reward of 500 dollars for my arrest. Two days later, I replied with an offer of 5,000 dollars to whoever arrested the governor: this reward was publicly posted on Saturday, November 27, 1813.

My prestige grew more after the publication of that reward. In that way I publicly notified my fellow citizens that I was not seeking celebrity but wished to establish a prosperous community by lowering the prices of consumer goods. I intended to ruin the system, then in effect, of the customs duties which fell heavily upon the merchandise seized and confiscated while exercising the recognized, legal practice of privateering against enemy ships.

The governor, vainly trying to crush my commune, took recourse to new methods. Maliciousness went into action. I then took several soldiers prisoner, brought them to my commune, and offered them nourishment, as well as a high wage. At the time of their liberation, I advised them to create disorder in the ranks of the army and ready themselves to defend their city as well as all the upper Mississippi valley.

My exhortations had some effect, but the politicians ignored this call to arms. The governor remained deaf to my cries of alarm and continued to seek new ways of arresting me, secretly setting up grand juries that issued indictments falsely accusing alleged pirates.

Remember that at that time, that is to say, toward 1812-1814, before the battles of New Orleans, there were not any American merchant vessels on the high seas. All the American ports were blockaded. After taking Detroit on August 15, 1812, and Washington on August 14, 1814, the English reduced the latter to ashes.

My officers were indicted for piracy. Army and navy detachments arrived in the commune of Grande Terre to make arrests and confiscate property. My brother Pierre was surprised by a group of soldiers and arrested on June 6, 1814, a Monday. Accused of piracy, he was secretly placed, hands and feet tied, in the depths of a dungeon. On July 18, 1814, a grand jury brought forth new indictments. On Monday, September 5, 1814, at two thirty in the morning, my brother Pierre escaped from the lice-ridden prison of the Cabildo.

In the meantime, the enemy continued to make me offers, trying to win me over to their side. The English knew that my fleet was superior to theirs on the high sea and that we had the most skillful cannoneers. They were still unaware of the existence of my land stores and the reserves of powder and musket flints.

After the escape of my brother Pierre, the American ship *Carolina* with the Forty-Fourth Infantry aboard and escorted by seven gunboats, landed at Grande Terre on Friday, September 16, 1814, at four o'clock in the morning to make arrests after the escape of Pierre from the Cabildo prison and his arrival at Grande Terre on Thursday, September 8, 1814.

I decided to visit Alexandre Labranche, who lived in the plantation of Saint Charles Parish more to the north. I then had to leave Grande Terre to inspect Caillou Pass. Order was given to my officers never to attack the American flag, but if an English warship approached the coast, without a flag of cease-fire or truce, my men of Grand Terre were to open fire immediately. I expected the arrival of the English fleet rather than that of the American ships, given that my officers had arrested the English captain Lockyer of the *Sophia*, a British warship and all its crew the morning of Friday, September 2, 1814. After holding and interrogating them for two days, we released them on Sunday, September 4, at sunset with the advice not to cross so far to the west of the southern pass.

If my officers in my absence were set upon by thieves who chanced upon them, they had an order to set the merchandise on fire. On land as on the open sea, I always had the motto: "war on pirates, whoever they may be;" for they too were only trying to make more sales for their gain in order to satisfy their own interests.

In regard to the day when Commodore D. C. Patterson and General G. T. Ross of the American Army landed at Grande Terre, I later learned that they had planned to confiscate ships and merchandise for their own and their families' personal use. However, my officers immediately seized torches and set fire to the vessels and warehouses. Six of my vessels burned: the *Wilgas*, *Véloce*,

Penwith, Spiritus, Success, and the *Pinar de Lucien.* Twenty-six others were taken to New Orleans: the *Casadora, Tigre, Non-telle, Surprendre, Genny, Guèpe, Bolívar, Melita, Mouche, Misère, Espion, Dorada, Harlequin, Petit-milan, Cometa, Fille de Golfe, Lune de Novembre, Esperanza, Amiable María, Luisa Antonio, Republica, Diligent, Flora Américain, Ponchita, Philanthrope,* and the *Prix-dernier.*

My elder brother and my staff officers were arrested and locked up as pirates in the lice-ridden Cabildo prison. Six hundred thousand dollars worth of merchandise were also taken off to New Orleans. General Ross left a guard of 50 soldiers at Grande Terre, but three of my vessels returned and took General Ross's garrison prisoner. We raided Barataria too. Militia soldiers taken by my men were to be released during the years that preceded the British invasion.

No one took as an active a part as I did in the defense of the territory. I had to combat the corruption of politicians in power and at the same time hold back the English by trickery and keep them from approaching our bays. The governor, undergoing pressure from numerous souls loyal to me in New Orleans, was beginning to grasp the gravity of the situation. My attorneys Mr. Livingston and Mr. Grymes went to court to request the liberation of my men and the restitution of the goods seized by Commodore Patterson of the American Navy and General Ross of the American Army. The two officers replied with a countersuit claiming my goods and considering themselves to have the right to them for their personal benefit.

In a letter to General Jackson on September 19, 1814, the governor boasted of having succeeded in destroying my first colony at Grande Terre and assured him that the area was safe from invasion. General Jackson was then garrisoned in Mobile. Now, the governor was unaware that I had other warehouses filled with rifles, powder, and cannons. The governor and General Jackson did not see to what degree my men were indispensable to the defense of Louisiana: they persisted in calling us bandits from hell and thieves.

They had to change their minds later, but following the advice of my lawyer, I made a point of obtaining a personal meeting with the governor. One day I entered his office without an invitation and even without warning him of my visit. I straight away explained to him my plans for defense and first of all described the gravity of the situation along the coast since the destruction of my colony and my fort by the very ones I wished to help. I dared the governor to have coffee with me; he refused. However, giving in to my threats, he agreed to no longer employ armed forces against me and my colonies and to accept my help: 1,162 men, rifles, powder, and 362 cannons and more than 400 expert cannoneers. He allowed us into New Orleans and to construct our barricades and ramparts ourselves. Mr. Livingston, my defense attorney, then wrote to President Madison, asking him for reinforcements to help us defend New Orleans, as well as soliciting the acquittal of several of my imprisoned officers.

Rumor had it that General Jackson would soon be on his way to New Orleans. However, my negotiations with the governor remained fruitless. I worked on other projects and stayed hidden in the city when I had business to conclude, and at the same time I led the continued privateering effort against England and Spain, disposing of cargoes as usual. So I kept busy, with a will of iron, despite lack of sleep and food, keeping an unshakeable fidelity to my adopted country, and seeing that my officers and soldiers remained in good condition and well informed about the events, and my other men continued my voyages.

As soon as the English discovered that my colony and fort at Grande Terre had been destroyed by fanatics, they realized that an entry to the United States was open. I brought the news to New Orleans that 15,000 elite English soldiers were leaving the Irish coast with the lower Mississippi as their destination and their mission the capture of New Orleans. Those troops left Ireland in mid September 1814. I was aware of all that concerned their movements and numbers, for I had their complete confidence.

I kept them from Grande Terre by invoking the troubled condition of the bay and the presence of American garrisons on the lower Louisiana coasts. I had good reason to keep them from the Grande Terre pass because of my warehouses loaded with musket flints, powder, and cannons. If the English had discovered and pillaged my warehouses, their invasion attempt would have been crowned by success; New Orleans would have fallen into their hands. They would have seized the upper Mississippi valley and provoked an uprising of all the Indian tribes in a victorious march toward the east, which would have pushed the United States into the Atlantic Ocean. The English wrote me letters to that effect, trying to win me over to their cause with several offers.

I began to lose patience with the alleged arrival of reinforcements coming from the north, under the command of General Coffee. I learned that General Coffee thought only of pillage, just like Commodore Patterson whose seizure of Grande Terre was worth 600,000 dollars in vessels and merchandise.

At that time, in November 1814, the governor thought he had reduced me to silence: several of my men were under lock and key; my colony had been ravaged; and I had lost my ships. During those two months he acted stupidly, insisting on not seeing the seriousness of the situation.

General Coffee, who at the head of regional troops made up of frontiersmen and planters arrived at that moment from the North, abandoned any thought of theft and pillage at my expense when a messenger warned him of the advance of the English forces; besides that, my men mounted a close guard of my merchandise.

Nevertheless, I continued to smuggle our privateering booty, using islands farther west as bases. That contraband proved later to be a disguised benefit, for the goods seized by me were as of much use as an avant garde unit. For his part, the governor a little later requested a pardon from President Madison, so as to calm the honorable citizens who had continued to do business with us.

What I was anxiously waiting for was the arrival of General Jackson. Rumor had it that he had left Mobile with New Orleans as his destination. Some of my intelligence officers left on reconnaissance to inspect his men's equipment: they reported to me that they were poorly equipped and very slow moving.

However, on Wednesday, November 30, 1814, the attention of the English camp of the La Ronde and Bienveneau plantations, which relied upon the protection of my secret line of artillery close by, was attracted by a naval maneuver of the enemy toward the east in Borgne Bay [sic].

On Thursday, December 1, 1814, I sent three emissaries to the English camp. One of them, Claude Hudspeth, began to speak out of line, doubtless under the effect of drink, which caused him to be taken prisoner along with the two others. On Saturday, December 3, 1814, I sent another group of messengers with the mission of finding why our comrades had been detained. It is at that time that the English realized we had changed sides, I and my forces at Barataria, to ally ourselves with the Americans.

The English were 12 kilometers southeast of New Orleans and were encamped at Bienveneau Plantation, and at the La Coste, Villeré , and La Ronde plantations. They numbered 14,660 well trained soldiers fresh from the Napoleonic campaigns.

The arrival of General Jackson on the first Thursday of December 1814 brought scant comfort to New Orleans and its environs. His appearance and that of his few soldiers in ragged uniforms caused widespread astonishment. According to custom, naturally, they normally met in the governor's office to discuss plans for fortifications and battery placements, and they proclaimed martial law. Their activities, very troubling at the beginning, caused a serious crisis in business and banking.

The silver of my commune was filed into bits that were used in place of coins: General Coffee's soldiers gave an ugly name to that custom I had. Today still in the place where I live I hear that same expression in terms of portions in pieces: "bits 'n pieces."

More and more I was losing patience with the conduct of the leading citizens of the city and with hearing lies and insults that were heaped upon me and my men. I could not waste any more time waiting for the opportunity that would put me face to face with General Jackson. Accompanied by some of my staff officers, I met the General on the northeast corner of Saint Philippe and Royal Streets. I explained to him my actions suffused with loyalty and patriotism that had no equal in the 38 years which had passed since the proclamation of American independence.

I challenged him to a duel in reply to the false, punishable insults that were addressed to us despite the respect I felt for his uniform. I must say that indeed the general seemed to me to be of an intelligence quite inferior to mine. He refused to answer my challenge; I threatened to slap his face; my elder brother then intervened to reconcile us.

The General received us in his office at 106 Royal Street and asked us for information on the enemy: the immediate defense measures that I suggested were accepted on Sunday, December 4, 1814.

Earlier, the loyalty of our attitude before General Jackson's arrival was made evident: my officers, freed from custody, received a full pardon, and were recognized as free men. They went to work at once, helped by my other Baratarians, and prepared the defense of the United States. This was the turning point of my career and the best moment of my life, the moment when I decided, once and for all, to chase the brutish English from American soil.

The English opened fire on the American gunboats on Wednesday, December 14, 1814, seizing five of the American naval vessels in three hours of combat. The sea defense of New Orleans was thus almost completely annihilated. General Jackson, who knew nothing about the strength of the English army and had only been in New Orleans for scarcely two weeks, was alarmed by the loss of American vessels. He prepared to request reinforcements while my secret agents prevented the English from advancing too rapidly.

I have had defeats but never illusions; with a common agreement, General Jackson and I resolved to try a daring move and attack the English simultaneously, with one of General Coffee's battalions and a battery of my cannoneers on Friday, December

23, 1814, at sunset. The battle lasted for almost three hours, and the losses were 18 times higher on the English side: we lost only 24 of our men.

After the English discovered my alliance with the American army, they tried to gain some time and find new positions to attack. As my mission was fulfilled in every way, I suggested that General Jackson visit several bays in Barataria and different places, the forts Saint Philippe, Petites Coquilles and the fort Petite Coquille to the northwest of New Orleans.

Reinforcements arrived for us from the state of Tennessee as well as from Creoles from all the regions of Louisiana. Indians were recruited and their services well paid. From Kentucky arrived three generals and 500 soldiers; New Orleans soon became a garrison town. All those soldiers arrived in New Orleans miserably dressed, without flints, and with very little powder. It was a horrible spectacle, above all for those like me who knew the number of British troops and their equipment. My magazines contained enough powder and flints to equip an army of 30,000 men if necessary.

On Wednesday, December 28, 1814, at Bienveneau Plantation, the English launched another attack that was repulsed with heavy losses on their side but insignificant ones on ours. On Friday, December 30, 1814, we could see the English digging trenches and cutting down trees. On Sunday, January 1, 1815, my proficient cannoneers opened fire on them at long range, destroyed their fortification plans, and killed a great number of their soldiers without touching one of ours.

On our side, we tried to protect ourselves with bales of cotton, but the bales became useless because fire was breaking out near our powder stores. I gave an order to my secret agents to deliver more flints, powder, and cannons. Mr. Arsène Lacarrière and I both sought different methods of protection against enemy fire. We chose a flat spot between the river and a marsh, not far from Dreux Plantation, to construct our fortifications made of earth and felled trees near Boisgevais Canal, made in a horseshoe shape to keep us hidden from the enemy. The greatest part of our work was done by feel in black night.

The night of the second of the month a pleasant banquet re-united General Jackson, Major Latour, and my captains. It was a very cordial evening; my brothers Alexandre and Pierre were both present. At two o'clock in the morning Pierre and I left for New Orleans. Mr. Latour and I took leave of General Jackson, leaving him sufficient reserves of flints, powder, and cannons and after organizing my artillery into sturdy batteries. I slowly made my way toward the city, stopping soldiers that I met on the road to ask them if they were well equipped.

I arrived in the city at four o'clock in the morning. Mr. Latour and I retired for a short rest. Messrs. Latour, Davezac, Villeré, Marigny, Roffignac, Nolte, Loailler, Latrobe, Claiborne, Blanque, and Livingston, and I spent the day of Tuesday, the third and Wednesday, January 4, 1815, helping many citizens evacuate the city.

On Thursday, January fifth we inspected Fort Petites Coquilles and Fort Saint Charles. Messrs Livingston, Villeré, Marigny, Davezac, and Claiborne returned to the city to accompany about 300 soldiers who came to establish a fortified position on the east bank of Lake Ponchartrain on Friday, January 6, 1815.

On Saturday, January 7, 1815, I was going to Barataria and the Temple to inspect the reserves of flint and powder; I returned to make my report to General Jackson and certified that all was finally in good order for crushing the British. I stayed with General Jackson until ten o'clock in the evening and then left on a mission at Fort Saint Charles.

The following day, Sunday, January 8, 1815, I was awakened from my sleep before dawn by an English attack. General Humbert crossed the river to take help to General Jackson. The same Sunday, January 8, while going to the rear of my artillery batteries without knowing who was retreating, I greatly feared that my supplies of flints and powder were exhausted. I heard the rumble of cannons raging in the distance; I was almost out of breath from running through the bushes and mud. My hands were bruised, my clothing torn and dirty, my feet soaked.

No one was more impatient than I to find my cannoneers that day in the early hours of the morning. Upon arriving in the lines, I could hardly believe the result of the battle. My brother Alexandre was the most expert shot of the battery; with a single shot he knocked General Pakenham from the back of his horse. The general died within two hours, his legs taken off. Never had I imagined that the combat would be of such short duration.

When we arrived, the spectacle presented before us by the battlefield was so horrible that we could not believe our eyes. General Jackson praised the troops' merit highly and marveled at the accuracy of the cannoneers' fire and that of Uncle Reyné, for it was they, with their precise fire, who had shot down the British officers and their horses.

I have to remember the great valor and loyalty that my cannoneers showed. François Rigaud helped my brother Alexandre and my Uncle Reyné, who commanded the batteries; and they were also dead from fatigue and lack of sleep and covered with mud from tramping in the marsh. The spectacle of those 3,000 dead Englishmen lying lifeless on the battlefield was horrible to see. Our own total losses did not reach 100 men. I lost six of my own men.

The retreating British kept firing at us, but without effect. That Sunday, New Orleans was awakened early to a loud firing that resounded like thunder and, espying a gleam looking like lightning, began to feel a strong foreboding of disaster. They closed their window shutters tight, locked the doors of all the buildings and houses, and fled in great numbers to the upper reaches of the river, fearing the English advance that was lugubriously described to them as taking away their wives and children, reducing their brothers and husbands to slavery, and tearing them from their homes.

At mid morning the first news was sent to the city to announce that our noisy cannons were the great victors of the battle.

A widespread rejoicing extended even to the officers and soldiers who were on the battlefield, which had become silent and clear of smoke toward noon.

Many people who had left the city in hysteria were skeptical and pessimistic at the thought that some spy had slipped into the city with false news. Toward the middle of the afternoon, people outside the city began to feel confident of their security and returned home. The reserve soldiers in the city began to form up on the *Place d'Armes* to celebrate the triumph and victory.

My brother Pierre was also a messenger in the artillery lines. He never felt very well after his time in prison during the stifling months of the summer of 1814 when he was kept in chains a part of the time.

Many artillerymen and I were acclaimed with the highest honors. My officers and I accepted the opportunity with good faith and without losing sight of the humanitarian work that awaited us. Personally, I was never a man to let anyone idolize my officers or me. No one was more impatient than I to administer medicine and dressings, night and day, to the sick and wounded. Many important people wanted me to spend the day in the city; I refused by assuring that the moment was not for rest or for pleasure.

Governor Claiborne, Mr. Jn Sauvinet, Mr. Ns. Girod, Mr. Ed. Livingston, Mr. Nolte, and I went to contribute to the charitable works of the Ursuline nuns. We spent every day on duty with the sick and the wounded soldiers from Monday, January 9 through Thursday, January 12, 1815.

So as not to linger in the uncertainty of waiting, we set to work on the subject of other matters of vital importance. That day, Saturday, January 14, 1815, my captains Rafel de Lisa, Jn. Little, Jn Leal de Franca, and Ernst Bramlit, in order to perfect a tactical plan and methods of capturing some of the English evacuating the territory or in retreat near Lake La Borgne, had the mission of seizing some of their sources of provisions. This was to be a compensation to the privateers at the mouth of Borgne Bay. Through skillful tactics to the east of the mouth, and on the open sea near

Chat Island, we seized two English ships without any resistance from them.

The English were short on food; they had many wounded on board their ships, which were retreating, and they surrendered with pleasure to our commands. We sent 340 prisoners to Cartagena. We handed over the two vessels to the cause of the Cartagena revolution. A part of the merchandise was unloaded at the mouth of the Calcasieu with the help of Mr. Arsène Lebleu.

On Saturday, January 21, 1815, I went to New Orleans. I arrived in the city at eight o'clock at night and retired to take a short rest. When I awoke at seven o'clock in the morning after ten hours sleep, I saw the *Place d'Armes* full of people: bands played the famous *Marseillaise,* and New Orleans resounded to the peal of bells. After great efforts the city of New Orleans had done everything necessary to assure its security and commerce in a very few days.

I added that I had sure evidence as proof that my privateers had seized two of their ships then, that these were leaving the Borgne Bay pass from the east near Chat Island with a lightened cargo and on board 340 prisoners whom they were hastening to abandon to the hands of my officers, happy to lighten their vessels at sea.

General Jackson and Governor Claiborne decided to organize the meeting of a committee to choose a day for a banquet, as well as a ball, for the celebration of the victory. Monday, January 23, 1815, was the day chosen for the parade and the victory ball. The *Place d'Armes* was the center of the gala, everyone, young and old, took part. Big bands played while leading the parade. Church bells rang in the whole city, cannon salvos were fired to celebrate the triumph, and it was the only day of my life to appear and be recognized by the general public. It was moving and cause for reflection, and a somewhat unusual feeling for me of great rejoicing, especially at seeing my two elder brothers and some of my officers lined up in the parade, the very ones who a few months before were in their prison of the Spanish commandant, dressed in rough clothing and accused of piracy, then liberated on the battle-field, and who annihilated the enemy and whom the public admired and praised with elegies and honor for their valor as expert cannoneers.

The streets were filled by the crowd; the day ended; many people dispersed and returned to their homes as night fell. The principal, eminent citizens met for the banquet and ball at the French chargé's house. My brothers excused themselves to return home at nine o'clock. Many other people encouraged me to stay for the ball afterward. I danced two dances. General Jackson and I attracted stares and were the most noticed; many ladies with their husbands asked each other many questions. The youngest ladies looked at me, questioned one another, and passed answers back and forth to each other. General Jackson and his officers were amused by it; they were filled with enthusiasm by the questions and answers.

That night pleased me greatly. It was my first time in such a large social event; I was completely unaccustomed to large crowds and kept my reserve during long conversations, limiting myself to reply very briefly to questions so as not to reveal my true personality or my privateering enterprises to everyone, for I was preoccupied at the thought of the enemy in retreat, who was boarding ship to leave the country. The night was ending; many began to leave before midnight. I left at two o'clock of that morning. I rose at a [forgotten] hour of the same morning.

                                                                Jn Laffite

AFTER THE BATTLE
OF NEW ORLEANS

Bethalto, Illinois, Monday, May 4, 1846

The afternoon of Thursday, January 26, 1815, my brothers with some of my officers went to visit General Jackson to discuss the subject of my property held by Commodore Patterson and General Ross. We went to the office of Governor Claiborne to discuss the case. Our meeting was of short duration due to the wait for additional information coming from Washington, which was undergoing repair and reconstruction from the results of the damage inflicted by the English in 1814.

The discussion concerning the holding of my property dragged on without end. My protest regarding my property was sent to Washington while I awaited the finding, or the future possibility of amnesty, after the proclamation issued for a full pardon by Governor Claiborne on December 17, 1814, and then sent to the President of the United States. Our meeting ended that day with few or no results concerning the property occupied by the high military command. Monday, February 20, 1815, the principals, my attorneys Messrs. Morel, Grymes, and Livingston disputed my seizures.

General Jackson's martial law, already in force in the city for a month, brought about discord and hatred and caused a crisis in business; its effects spread throughout the state.

I soon discovered the plots of Governor Claiborne, and actions of Judge Dominic Hall, and Commodore Patterson and General Ross on February 22, 1815. It was in that period of early March

1815 when the plots of General Jackson, who with them ignored the rights of citizens and acted as absolute masters and caused a large number of prominent citizens of New Orleans, state legislators, and important planters, to begin to raise protests and demand the end of martial law. I spoke in their name several times to General Jackson in favor of the end to martial law.

He replied to me, alleging that he was not sure the English had completely evacuated the region and that he feared a new invasion. I explained to General Jackson, several judges, and many others that the English had completely abandoned the territory and there was no reason to fear a new invasion. I added that I had convincing proof in that my privateers had captured two of their ships as they were leaving the east pass of Lake Borgne with a reduced cargo and 340 prisoners whom they hurried to hand over to my officers, happy to lighten their ships on the high sea.

The complaints and protests against martial law increased. The English having left Louisiana, French elements had the impression that for the General, the law was only a pretext to exercise his authority over them. That law remained in vigor until March 14, 1815, and caused serious distress. Many soldiers deserted to return home. Others emigrated to the still untamed western territories.

The leading businessmen of the city and the mayor Nicolas Girod himself began to feel irritation and displeasure. The court martial made numerous arrests. Consternation grew among the French-speaking populace, which soon asked for the publication of a notice urging those who had been banished to return to obtain their pardon and have legal recourse before Louisiana's civil courts while avoiding military tribunals. General Jackson, irritated by the unwarranted demands for his resignation began to claim that they were worthless and improperly written. He ordered all the French, including the French Consul, to leave the city.

During the second half of February 1815, anxiety in regard to the English who had evacuated the city spread rapidly among the people. Mr. Cotton, publisher of the gazette *Courier of Louisiana*, published a British peace treaty on Tuesday, February 28, 1815, thereby soothing the widespread uneasiness by affirming that all danger had passed.

General Jackson was angered by it and had the publisher arrested. He told the General that the author of the article was none other than Mr. Louis Louaillier, a member of the Louisiana Legislature who had taken an active role in the defense of the United States. General Jackson maintained that the English had not made peace when they took over a small fort near Mobile on February 12, 1815. He took advantage of the capture to order Mr. Louaillier's arrest. He was arrested at the Maspero Bank on Sunday, March 5, 1815, and locked up in the military prison. The judge of the United States Court of Appeals granted *habeus corpus* to Mr. Louaillier.

General Jackson exploded in anger; he had Judge Hall arrested: on Tuesday, March 7, 1815. That same day, the court martial judged Mr. Louaillier, accused of espionage for having incited the people to disobedience, insubordination, and mutiny, and , finally, for having illegally violated the martial law. He was acquitted. General Jackson's anger turned into delirium. The General had foreseen the trial's outcome; he refused to release him, but instead had Judge Hall and Mr. Louaillier sent from the city on March 10, 1815.

Three days later on Monday, March 13, 1815, a few cannons were fired to announce and transmit the news of the peace treaty signed by the President of the United States, which ordered the pardon of all convicted soldiers. The French Consul and the French returned, clearly expressing their scorn for General Jackson. Tuesday, March 14, 1815, the General, receiving orders, suspended martial law. Judge Hall and Mr. Louaillier, both freed, also returned to the city. Public opinion had already changed, interest lost in the general; French anger reached its height. After the end of martial law, civil courts received suits against General Jackson accusing him of disregard for citizens' rights and disrespect for the law. Found guilty, he was sentenced to a 1,000 dollar fine. Strong emotions prevailed that day at the court's doors, where a populace

ready for violence gathered. Many of my officers were there, still
loyal and attached to General Jackson. They cheered him in the
reception hall, reducing the crowd to silence and maintaining order. My brother Alexandre proposed a collection to pay the fine;
General Jackson was filled with joy by that and wept tears of re-
pentance. He refused, but stated that he insisted absolutely upon
replying some day to that generous offer. Thirty years later the
General was to be granted a restitution of the 1,000 dollars with
interest, a total of 2,700 dollars, by the United States government.

Mr. Andrew Jackson died 11 months ago: some personal comments regarding him: I was fond of him. He was energetic but
always imagined the worst. I describe General Jackson as I knew
him without condemnation or any judgment about his past. At
the time he and I were both in New Orleans, many years ago, he
had not yet become President of the United States. On his arrival
in New Orleans he was sick. He was a man possessed of a double
personality, both optimistic and pessimistic. During peace he could
love and hate almost at the same instant. In wartime, for him all
the means he sought justified the end. He was not perfidious but
overly cautions. He was somewhat jealous and melancholy, and
did not easily admit to a mistake he had made. He had a good,
practical mind; sometimes disturbing, causing things to be done
contrary to his original intentions. Changing his mind
pronouncedly, he claimed to be satisfied with the results. He had
an excellent, good disposition but did not know how to apply it to
make everyone appreciate it at the most crucial moment.

As for me, I was not with him after the battles; he was personally occupied with his entourage of officers. I had little respect,
faith, or confidence toward those subordinate officers. I had a fair
amount to do to place my own men in a new stance. My property
remained seized by the two officers, Commodore Patterson and
General Ross of the army.

Personally, I did not have time to interfere in military affairs. I
had never served in a land army before the war against the English.
My only work had kept me busy at sea. I had a vast, powerful fleet,

and I was still resolved to fight against Spain and England. I had counted on the help of some good men in the interior of the Union to launch me on the high seas with some of my vessels against England. To my regret, my illusions were never a reality. Everything began to go wrong and turn against me in the near term.

General Jackson would have taken command if he had been approved by Washington. He hated the English because of the damage caused by their invasions of Washington in August 1814, and Detroit on August 16, 1812, and of Louisiana, the blockade of other sea ports, and because of the many American citizens who had never been freed from England to return to America.

I can attest with certainty that I discovered General Jackson and his staff officers were secretly plotting many deceitful schemes against me. At the time when, after the Battle of New Orleans, martial law had been in effect for two months, I noticed that under certain influences the General was beginning to take secret measures like dictating bellicose orders and secret imprisonments. He was excessively emotional and also inclined to a mental defect of forgetting past favors. The very valuable contributions that I had brought him were to fall into neglect and be forgotten: never did the War Department of Washington record it.

General Jackson and his staff left after stuffing their bags, with the full authorization to take away several of my cannons and a quantity of powder and flints. President Madison and General Jackson neglected to enumerate the materiel that I had provided them and give precise figures: 366 cannons; 6,400 kilos of powder; 1,720 kilos of flints, about 300,000 of them, 800 men at the battle; 315 at other positions along the Louisiana coast to the east of Bayou La Fourche; and 400 skillful cannoneers at war 12 kilometers to the southeast of New Orleans close to Bienveneau Plantation.

I often wonder, after the 32 years that have passed since, what would have happened if I had switched sides and accepted the promises of the English. The name of General Jackson and all his staff officers would have tumbled into oblivion, just like that of

General Winder, beaten by the English in Washington during August in the summer of 1814. President Madison, the members of his cabinet, and all the officials of the era, would have taken flight toward the west under false names or would have surrendered.

Whether I am at home or traveling, I have always up to the present day, had the great flag of the United States displayed, and I have always cherished and revered it with all the respect it is due. The United States would have been crushed and entirely eliminated from the face of the earth almost 39 years after winning its independence.

In the form of a proclamation dated February 6, 1815, in Washington, and received in New Orleans on Tuesday, February 28, 1815, President Madison published a notice of pardon for the good and loyal services rendered by me and my men as patriots. My officers and I highly appreciated and accepted in good faith the proclamation of total pardon for past crimes given by President Madison. The details were very interesting, but it scarcely had any value and was made up of good, but empty words. First of all, we never were the pirates that we were accused of being. Our only crime was smuggling merchandise contrary to outrageous customs duties and revenue laws. This proclamation sounded very hollow and contained no mention of the material aid that I had furnished, not only to defend the city of New Orleans but to prevent the destruction of the entire American Union by an invasion which, after having gone up the Mississippi, would have extended to the east—-as was the intention of the English. This proclamation was made out in legal terms but was not sufficiently official for me to give it entire credit.

I never want to possess the portrait of an official elected through venal methods. That person is very dangerous, and those practices applied to the lowliest justice officials will sooner or later lead a healthy nation into oblivion.

An inventor or a great donor is always prey to the persecutions of the rapacious. My three attorneys, Messrs. Livingston, Grymes, and Morel, quickly set about bringing lawsuits in court demanding the restitution of my property seized and held by Commodore Patterson and General Ross. The matter remained without issue for some time. That delay alerted the two officers and gave them the opportunity to put my goods up for auction. I was alarmed by their secret plots and quickly had my vessels repurchased through my agent and financier Mr. Jn Sauvinet and had him make bids. I employed Mr. Jn Blanque, Mr. Noël, Mr. Nolte, Mr. E.B. Jones, Mr. J.B. Arnaud, Mr. Jn. L. Leclerc, Mr. A. Davezac, and Mr. Jn Roffignac, and several others for bids of less importance. The majority of the merchandise was sold at a low price, which I completely approved. The great part of the populace of New Orleans greatly needed that merchandise.

The two officers also held on to small quantities of gold and silver, but they placed no precious metal for sale and failed to send any to the Treasury in Washington either but, rather, kept it for their personal use and spent it wildly.

Those sales took place on Tuesday and Wednesday May 2 and 3, 1815. The auction, which took place despite the lawsuit, weighed heavily on the minds of my attorneys and me. After causing the suit to drag on, it was sent to the Supreme Court in Washington. I left New Orleans on Wednesday, October 25, 1815, to appear in person in Washington.

During the tense days that preceded the outcome of the affair, while waiting for the results of the trial, I took several trips, leaving Washington several times for Philadelphia and Baltimore and went two times to Charleston, South Carolina. I had a lot of business to do, especially concerning a vessel in the Baltimore shipyard.

I spent some time with my old father and my youngest sister Yvonne, and I also visited the homes of Mr. Guestier and Mr. Destillieu. I had one of my ships repaired in Philadelphia and from there went several times to visit Mr. Joseph Bonaparte on the other side of the river to discuss with him the question of French refugees and draw up escape plans for his brother, whom the English were keeping prisoner on Saint Helena. At Charleston I had a large ship under construction, which was to be larger, faster, with better batteries of pivoting cannons than the English or Spanish could employ.

My trial in Washington was not ending as well as my attorneys had expected. Despite the fact that I did not urgently need what I wanted to regain, I nevertheless persistently remained faithful to my principles, determined to have recourse to the law and obtain the just return of my property and wanting to reveal the culpable and bring them to justice.

My attorneys informed me that the trial would be long and, doubtless after remaining pending, would simply disappear, and that for several reasons the real value of my goods was neither registered nor known; and other merchandise had been added to mine at the auction organized by Ross and Patterson. This extra merchandise was supposed to have belonged to a well known Creole lady, who one day had left New Orleans, never to return. At the time the city authorities did not reveal her name or identity to me.

There were, and there still are to this day, a large number of wealthy residents of New Orleans and vicinity to whom I gave up a quantity of jewels, for it was always the jewels that received the lowest offers in all my sales, to such an extent that I made gifts of them to poor people.

Antoine Arcas on April 25, 1814, made a claim at a local court in regard to the theft of the cargo of his ship *Lanisa Antonio* in the month of May 1813, which opened a new dossier of complaints against me. The chief accountant and the verifications that I had at Grande Terre and Barataria never uncovered any merchandise in my warehouses fitting the descriptions that he gave. As well, they failed to find any jewels or silk goods belonging to the Creole lady . . .

That auction was simply a carefully mounted operation to create a diversion and cause the withdrawal of my lawsuit as well as further disseminate the insulting name of pirate. Many highly placed people in new Orleans and vicinity placed in doubt the authenticity of those acts of piracy. But the sinister story circulated from mouth to mouth and caused critical or incredulous voices to be raised.

I openly invited several to interpret the meaning of the word pirate in slang, warning them to hold their tongue just as I had warned many others before the invasion that I would accept no more insults. Through error, the name of pirate, which became strongly anchored in the minds of most people before the British invasion, was whispered in every corner for some time among the gossips, a name that I have always hated. My privateers and I were never pirates; we were never guilty of such an act. Our privateering enterprise was a legitimate business under the orders of marque.

However, it overwhelmed my attorneys and was a cause for the suit in Washington failing to succeed, all while making me foresee the future in the darkest light. My men and I never dreamed that those whom we had defended would have sought to obtain such a result and that the justice of the country would have been transformed and rendered into a travesty to allow a secret minority of the privileged to bring about the triumph of their selfish cause.

I remained intermittently in Washington from the day of my arrival on Tuesday, November 7, 1815, until Sunday, March 3, 1816.

Jean Laffite

Saint Charles, Friday, May 29, 1846

Today and the day before yesterday I visited Mr. U.M. Campbell in the city of St. Charles, Missouri.

On Wednesday, December 27, 1815, I wrote a letter to President Madison. The stay in Washington and those trips brought me many new ideas and projects while I awaited the verdict which would decide the fate of my property. The nation was heavily in debt. Concerning itself, there had been no claim voted in regard to the English for the damage inflicted by them between the years 1812-1815.

The President and his cabinet found themselves facing such a national treasury deficit that they felt obliged to undertake immediate measures and conclude peace treaties if they wanted to strengthen maritime commerce and get it started again. There was something strange in those rapid changes of course and the conclusion of peace treaties with yesterday's enemy. Many Americans did not approve of that attitude, and personally it hardly pleased me, but I could do nothing. I was not a Virginia politician and did not belong to that clique.

I was all powerful on the sea but was bereft of any military force on land. I was still at war with England and Spain. I found that my future hopes concerning the unity of America were weakened after the victory at New Orleans and weakened even more a year later while I was in Washington.

Spain sent a representative, Mr. Luis De Onis, first to New Orleans then to Washington. He was an active man, and his reputation was not long in spreading after the secret meetings he held about commercial treaties.

My attorneys' men again explained to me that if I continued to fulfill my privateering mission and if I helped the revolutionaries of the province of Texas and Mexico against Spain, in the future I would have to contend with armed bands led by so-called generals, who would put my communes in danger and force me to accept some compromises.

I kept that warning in mind after I left Washington. I had also given my officers the task of beginning operations in the great state of Texas and Mexico, of watching the coast, establishing colonies for the French refugees, and preparing defensive fortifications against Spanish power. The income of the privateers' prizes was as great as before the English invasion.

My financial condition was only known a little later, but if I had been without money or clear means of supporting myself, I would have been reduced to begging in the street with an empty basket and without anything to show on the lapel of my coat but a wooden medal. Some 14 months after the victory parade on

January 23, 1815, the question of my goods taken by Commodore Patterson and General Ross still had not been decided in Washington.

In the month of April 1816, I decided to pursue my privateering on the high seas with the goal of weakening England and Spain and paralyzing their attacks against North and South America at the same time. This was done under the authority of letters of marque. My licensed vessels brought in captured enemy ships, and our seizures began to attain sizable proportions.

Since the death of my grandmother, I have taken at age 22, the principles she gave me as a rule of conduct in what I have done: "In high opposition to defeat Human Bondage."

The situations predicted were soon to become reality and lasted until the time when I was forced to burn the city of Galveston rather than hand it over to traffickers who were capable neither of fighting Spain nor building anything themselves.

Spain and England never intended to liberate their colonies and provinces. The English would never have acquired mastery of the seas if, during the period of the war of 1812 to 1815, the United States had granted privateer licenses to help their small warships in their naval struggle against the English.

I thought that before the landing of the English in Louisiana, General Jackson would have been court-martialed and would lose his rank of general because of the orders that he received from the Secretary of War when he took the initiative of fighting the Spaniards in Pensacola, Florida, during the summer and autumn of 1814, and used up his munitions while sickness weakened his tiny army.

Half of his 2,800 men and he were sick, his men without powder or musket flints. He arrived in New Orleans in December 1814 not knowing where the adversary had landed nor that they were five times his force.

The information that my officers and I furnished Mr. Jn Blanque, Arsène Latour, and numerous Frenchmen allowed Jackson to keep his prestige in a nation which survived as the victor over the "beasts."

Mr. Latour served first as a clerk and interpreter for General Jackson. Later he was promoted to a higher rank and was in charge of the disposition of the armies on the strategic positions in the outskirts of New Orleans. Sam Williams from the state of Rhode Island was himself promoted to the rank of administrative colonel and took Latour's place in Jackson's army. Sam Williams had also previously been one of my commune's clerks.

My officers and I were the only ones with in-depth knowledge of the effects of the tides on the waters of the bayous washing the thick forests located between the ocean and New Orleans. My men lived permanently in those low areas of Louisiana: they were the descendants of the first French who emigrated from France and settled in the southern region of Louisiana between the years 1720 and 1740.

General Jackson knew nothing of Louisiana geography: Arsène Latour, nothing of the geography of the lowlands. Jn Humbert helped Arsène Latour in regard to the area around New Orleans. Mr. Humbert was a soldier who had come from France: he had served under Napoleon Bonaparte, and he had similarly stirred up several revolts against the Spanish armies in the province of Texas during the period preceding the battles of New Orleans in December 1814 and January 1815.

The English were the great victors in the wars against Napoleon. Their prestige had grown, and they had acquired total latitude to pressure smaller, weaker nations through their commercial treaties. England and Spain both created great turmoil in Washington. The American officials of the era only concentrated on nations with which they had made Atlantic commercial treaties. Those principal nations were yesterday's rivals: England and Spain. The Washington officials neglected the best opportunities before them to explore the unknown, densely forested regions of western Louisiana Territory, which former President Jefferson had planned to do when he bought the area from France in April 1803 for the ridiculous sum of 15,000,000 government dollars. President Jefferson was far from suspecting that 15 years later the failure of his plans would be due to the influence of the European conflict between Napoleon and England.

One must also fault the blunders and negligence of the officials in power who imposed their will on the French refugees and refused them any right to emigrate and colonize the new Louisiana Territory. Those Washington officials who had nothing but empty bags in their hands turned their backs on the West and obstinately persisted in only worrying, from the Atlantic to the West, about their old enemy, England. Without a doubt, during that period Washington officials worked hard into the night to construct, reconstruct and repair damage from the English along the Atlantic coast, but they were off on the wrong track, and that mistake several years later caused the start of new disorders and a great deal of discontent in the country's interior.

The confusion reigning in Washington at that time, the way my lawsuit was neglected as the Supreme Court let it languish, the influence of the Spanish ambassador Luis De Onis, all led my brothers and me to create a secret organization in New Orleans. With a triple goal we aimed first at having significant amounts of money spent by the Spanish governor of Havana under the pretense of helping the Spanish authorities defend Texas, secondly, to continue to send out our privateering vessels while changing the names of their captains based on letters of marque coming from five different nations; third, we decided to arrest and get rid of those who were trafficking as they wished and exploiting the Indian tribes of the interior. (The Spanish and the English exploited the Indians for three centuries without obtaining good results.) Our program had for its fitting motto: "Construct, Explore, Colonize" the immense territories that opened before us without constraining the Indian tribes forced from their country of origin with the single goal of realizing a profitable expansion of our territory.

Luis De Onis, the Spanish ambassador to Washington, was a strong willed man full of cunning. He was to cause a certain amount of confusion to occur. Because of his ruses, Washington officials left unfinished what in the following years would cause still more disorder in the Union. Upon my arrival in New Orleans after my departure for Washington, I realized that De Onis had set up plans with the goal of turning several leaders of the Mexican Revolution away from their duty. The army of the Spanish king was strong: a great number of the officers at the head of the movement were executed after being taken prisoners. At the beginning of the first revolt led by the priest Hidalgo, who was executed by the Spaniards in October 1810, F. Morelos took the leadership of the revolt. He suffered several reversals and he too was taken prisoner after having set up the first Mexican Congress in the beginning of 1813. He was executed in Mexico City in 1815.

Jean Laffite

THE GALVESTON COMMUNE

Saint Louis, Monday, June 8, 1846

Mr. Humbert, one of my principal officers, who had been a head-strong man, had taken measures to take charge himself of the initiative of participating in the negotiations and giving credence to certain rebel generals who committed a great deal of fraud and wasted their personal profits on the superfluous. This was the cause for the defeat of General Humbert and his small army by the Spanish royalists.

My brother Alexandre furnished General Anaya with 2,200 kilograms of powder in April 1814, with the intention of new preparations for Texas operations. Therefore, the 2,200 kilograms were expedited to General Toledo. In the past General Humbert was an active man through his aid to General Toledo in the operations against the Spanish royalists of Texas.

General Humbert had 470 men in the field and 500 in reserve. General Toledo was exigent: he wanted everything at his disposition from one day to the next. Toledo encountered defeat everywhere: he was not the man needed, like General Humbert. General Toledo unleashed, with or without orders, an attempted attack against the Spanish garrison of Texas. His troops and those of General Humbert were defeated by an enemy superior in number and suffered heavy losses. After the defeat he complained to the priest Sedella that those soldiers hidden in ambush, who had fired on him and his men, were wearing the uniform of the Spanish Army but speaking English. General Toledo later disappeared mysteriously and was never heard of again.

General Humbert was a prescient and an able man with a lively mind, knowing how to act prudently before taking the initiative once he had been alerted. He hated lies and corrupting plots like those that Mr. De Onis had tried to use on him, above all at the time when the French with Napoleon were undergoing a period of reversals. In that year, 1813, the English began to invade the sea ports of the United States. I met General Humbert during a birthday dinner at his house, where my officers and I had been invited in New Orleans. My brothers, some of my officers, and I took good note of the advice of General Humbert and the priest Sedella and decided to take them into account in our future actions.

Means of transport were uncertain at that period, and the mail was problematic. Many of my officers were committed to defending the cause of Mexican independence. Great confusion arose among them in regard to letters that were stolen or misdirected. My brothers and I decided to convoke three other officers and met the next Tuesday, April 9, 1816.

The priest Sedella was never in favor of the English government or the government of the United States. As has been established previously, it was revealed behind closed doors that my brother Pierre and I were again to be caught in a trap, and upon my arrival in New Orleans, the priest De Sedella confirmed it. I began to understand that everything was true and boded ill.

The priest De Sedella gave me information that provided me with a solid basis for work. He informed me that many priests supported Mexican independence but maintained that the entire people must not rebel and dearly win that independence so that just a few other individuals might make bad use of it for their personal benefit. The priest De Sedella furnished me many materials: he knew the number of bandits who were getting ready to come in gangs to grab the profits of the Texas Revolution. He spoke to me about some defeated revolutionary generals who, after many misfortunes, had abandoned the cause of independence.

During our meeting we decided to give up all our plans for a heavily armed revolution in Mexico. We were to work for our cause from within, penetrate the Spanish Army, win over their generals to our cause, grab armaments for ourselves, and confiscate vessels, all under different names written upon our letters of commission.

My Uncle Reyné suggested and advised that my two elder brothers Alexandre and Pierre and I go see the priest De Sedella in New Orleans to combine information on the means and methods of establishing a new seaport where vessels would arrive and from which they would set out again without any risk on their own account or even from the Spanish royal armies.

Mr. Jn Picornell was the first to resign from the Council for Mexican Independence on February 12, 1814. He agreed to fight against the insurrection and received a position under Spanish control. Mr. Picornell was at one time a partisan of Mexican independence. For many reasons he resigned from the council to accept a position available in Havana under the Spanish government with the goal of suppressing any insurrection in Mexico and Texas. He announced his abandon of the cause of Texas and Mexican independence while claiming that some English agents as well as certain independent, conservative Americans had infiltrated the business under false pretense with the goal of profiting from Latin American independence.

He stated that the Americans of Virginia deserved no consideration nor gave an adequate reason to invade, intervene, or be concerned about Spain's American provinces, for they had previously neglected and not concerned themselves about exploring their own immense Louisiana Territory in search of mineral riches in the soil that President Jefferson, third President of the United States, had bought very cheaply from France in 1803. Mr. Picornell was an expert in history and psychology, and no one doubts that he was careful not to commit himself to the past as far as errors, mistakes of negligence, or inadvertence of others are concerned.

He stated that under President Madison Americans had neglected to establish a team of technicians to attempt, as Thomas Jefferson had intended, to have emigrants toward the West, so as

to spread out within the interior of the United States' own frontiers, instead of blindly taking part in the changing commercial
traffic to the east on the entire Atlantic Ocean and all that without
any guarantee or protection, only to be captured by the English,
who hated the American Declaration of Independence.

Mr. Picornell claimed that President Madison and his congress had acted very blindly when in June 1812 they declared war
on the English, who possessed the most important war fleet on the
high seas while the United States had only a very small number of
warships, and all that without any mandate for privateers, who
would have helped them in a naval combat that could have once
and for all caused the English Navy to lose its dominance of the
high seas.

Mr. Picornell under President Monroe recognized the principles when the initiative of protecting Latin America was voted.
Mr. Picornell then began to work undercover in secret against Spain,
which he had intended to keep current concerning insurrections
and revolts. Mr. Picornell was assigned to negotiate in Havana, Cuba,
concerning secrets and to negotiate with Alexandro Ramírez and General Cienfuegos and Governor De Cagigal. On February 12, 1814,
Mr. Picornell was replaced by General José De Herrera, named President of Mexico and Texas. Mr. Latour and Mr. Picornell were always
on duty to keep British agents away from the Mexican revolts.

Several meetings took place in New Orleans during 1816. We
elected Mr. Latour as the chief supervisor. He was to take the borrowed name of John Williams when he dealt with the English-
speaking population. He was named to the command of the vessel
Carmelita.

Our first meetings in the presence of the priest De Sedella
took place on Friday, August 6, 1813. General Humbert brought
up the subjects of the question of the emigration of French refugees and of the intervention in the affairs of Texas and the development of the revolution in Mexico. In that year, 1813, Spain was in
a weakened condition where the wars with Napoleon had plunged it.

After the English evacuation of January 1815 and my return

from Washington in the first days of spring 1816, our meetings began to take place regularly in New Orleans. General Picornell (Picornelli was his real name) was the first after General Humbert to meet the priest De Sedella at a later date, December 3, 1813 [sic]. The goal of the meeting was to organize the open struggle for Mexican independence against the Spanish royalists. General Picornell was to remain president of the Council of Mexico until new orders, barring any changes within the assemblies. Mr. Picornell, present at the meeting, gave his resignation from the presidency of the Council of Mexico and was named an assistant in the secret service on February 12, 1814. There was much at stake beyond Mexico and Texas. The province of Florida, another Spanish possession, was an additional subject of discussion which was addressed in New Orleans during the year 1817.

General Js Wilkinson of the United States Army appeared before the priest De Sedella as a bearer of information concerning bandits. If the general worked under the control of Spain, it was because he disapproved of the way that Washington negotiated with Spain. General Wilkinson kept us current about incursions planned into Texas by new organized gangs from Virginia, Kentucky, and Tennessee. General Wilkinson was filled with aversion for many of the military leaders from those states due to the fact that they continued to esteem England and its king and, furthermore, they belonged to the Tory element, which was ignorant of all things American and acted as secret agents in concert with the mother country with the goal of taking over Texas.

To be able to operate according to secret plans and stay in contact with those vile bandits, we adopted a secret code. General Wilkinson became number 13. My brother Pierre became 13-1 A. I had the number 13-2 R. My brother Alexandre, who was to remain on a permanent secret mission to New Orleans, had for his number 13-D. General Benito De Ariza had the number 45-V. General Arsène Latour was 7-C. Doctor Pierre Gual, an attorney living in Cartagena, had D- 4 for his number. That of the attorney Ed Livingston was B-7 and that of the attorney Jn Grymes, H-11.

The Generals Abner Duncan and Manuel Moreno had respectively for numbers A-5 and F-6. The latter was named Secretary in Buenos Aires, Argentina, and later designated governor when Florida was seized from Spain. David de Forrest was number 17-D. He was sent on a mission to meetings in Washington. François Dupuis, whose number was 17-J, was given a post in New Orleans near my brother Alexandre. Jn Tucker had F-19 as a number. Jn Desfarges F-7, Robert Johnston F-9, Jn West F-2, Joseph Bonaparte, who had taken the name of Jules Arceneaux, had F-13 for a number. He was to remain secretly near the city of Philadelphia with the goal of helping French refugees and colonists.

In Europe, after the struggle between Napoleon and England, poverty was widespread. After the defeat of Napoleon, King Ferdinand regained the Spanish throne on November 28, 1815. Spain began to reorganize, but it had few opportunities for expansion after the disappearance of its provinces of South America, all struggling for independence.

Mr. Latour had studied maps of the province of Texas. Ambassador De Onis in Washington began to discover our plans in regard to Texas and Florida. The cabinet of President Madison was constantly badgered by the Spanish ambassador, De Onis, concerning French immigrants and refugees. The United States was still in the cradle. There was no local justice to limit the acts of rich individuals.

British agents were numerous and active in the North. The United States did not have a very efficient secret service to work in the interior of the country at that moment when the Spanish agents were everywhere, but they were not as numerous in the North. It was easy to corrupt them, also by telling them that their language was marvelous. Certain of our agents were also secretly turned, led into error, and never came back. We did the same thing in the interior of the country to the British and Spanish agents: certain ones seemed very easy to capture so as to hide their identity and obtain information about our system in the interior. We were completely aware of their subversive methods, and they were never as free to return to their superiors.

The treaty with Spain had set the Sabine River as the frontier line, which caused great difficulty for the two sides, mine and the officials in Washington, to understand the problem of French colonization. Ambassador De Onis was very energetic. He even displayed a very great activity since the king of Spain had regained his throne after Napoleon's defeats. He caused several missteps by certain officials of Washington in regard to the provinces of Texas and Florida.

When they were very busy, I was as well—with my business in Galveston as well as with the captains' missions for the vessels at sea. My brother Pierre and Mr. Picornell differed in opinion on many points of view regarding projects because of strayed letters that had been falsified with additions by Ambassador De Onis' agents.

This was the beginning, or the start, of the suspicion caused by some of my officers. This made our privateering methods more zealous against Spain. José Manuel De Herrera was elected Consul of Mexico by my new assembly presided over by the priest De Sedella. He had been, at a certain time, an officer of my commune of Grande Terre. He was the same kind of man as General Toledo, Colonel Henri Perry, and Felipe Fortio, all active officers who constantly violated discipline and followed their own counsel, which put my communes in danger. They had no patience and angered at the least delay. At the beginning of our meetings under the presidency of the priest De Sedella, we tried to divide and incite the officials in Washington to break diplomatic relations with Spain. Our attempts were secret and not directed at the city of Washington. Our main project was to furnish surplus merchandise in our stocks to three vessels of the United States.

Abner L. Duncan and Jn West were the skippers who set sail to come to the aid of the Mexican rebels, but at sea they encountered superior Spanish forces near Vera Cruz and lost two vessels and a schooner, stirring up and almost causing a suspension or break in diplomatic relations between Spain and the United States. The vessel *Dos Hermanos* withdrew from battle with light damage.

A dossier was compiled of the letters exchanged between our committee at New Orleans and the Spanish governor of Havana, Cuba, and his subordinates. After being kept for 158 days it was burned. During our later meetings toward February 1815, we prepared the escape of Napoleon Bonaparte from his English prison on the island of Saint Helena.

Straight away we sent three vessels on a mission under the command of my eldest brother Alexandre, my Uncle Reyné, Captain Jn Brossière, my brother-in-law Laurent Maire, Mr. De Franca, Rafael Lisa. We received financial support from Jn Sauvinet, Jules Thiacus, Calvin Hillman, Nicolas Girod, and Mr. Garrot. On April 15, 1817, our assembly elected a new Mexican parliament. Mr. Louis Ituribarría was named, as well as a new general staff. Jn Ducoing left his business to join the administrative personnel of the commune.

As secret service officers I had Pierre Rousselin, Louis Durieux, Antoine Pironeaux, Ramon Espagnol, Bartholomé Lafon, Jn Fannette, Gregory McGregor, Elias Beanne, Nicolas Roquette, Uncle Reyné, Jn Giovanni, Js De LaPorte, Louis De Aury, Jn Thiacus, François de Rieuvre, Arsène Latour. And Angel Benito De Ariza, secret agent at New Orleans, was also in charge of the Spanish prisoners in Galveston.

Doctor Pierre Gual was a secret agent close to my Uncle Reyné for Venezuela and had the mission of helping in the affairs concerning the emigration of the French refugees arrived at the south pass of the Mississippi on July 17, 1816. He was dissuaded from coming into Louisiana in order to advise him to go secretly with Uncle Reyné to Venezuela and from there to other regions. Our assemblies continued in good order at New Orleans, and the oral accounts that we received from observers from Texas were excellent.

Louis De Aury, General L'Allemand, and General Bolívar were chosen to watch over the transport of the French refugees and their colonization. General Bolívar was always chosen first, General De Aury second, and General L'Allemand third.

General De Aury was chosen for the Ile du Serpent, also named Ile Saint Louis,* and planned for the French colonists. His mission was then changed; he was given orders to transport the French refugees to other regions. We tried to use the old Ile Saint Dominique, but the attempts at colonization did not work out there. We named General L'Allemand in his stead and to replace General De Aury at the Ile du Serpent, also called Saint Louis. General L'Allemand saw his colonial work crowned with success. The ambassador of Spain in Washington, Luis De Onis, raised inflamed protests against the French immigrants, claiming that Texas was still a Spanish province.

His distrust, always on the alert regarding our methods of resistance only grew. Our methods yielded excellent results. In Washington and New Orleans a few rare businessmen, unable to do business with us, plotted furtively against us. They were under the influence of De Onis, the ambassador to Washington.

Jn Laffite

Edwardsville, Wednesday, October 7, 1846

My main supervisors were Jn Grymes, Abner Duncan, Edouard Livingston, and my brother Pierre: they chose to attack Pensacola secretly. Pierre and Jn Welsh were the first to execute that project, but the Spanish royalists discovered the plot.

Our payments arrived in significant amounts from the governor of Havana. We were deceiving the governor by claiming that I was buying vessels with the goal of helping the Spanish royalists, but under cover my officers held Spaniards in my prison of Galveston.

---

* Ile du Serpent, Ile Saint Louis, Galveston and Campeche are all different names for the same island south of present day Houston, Texas.

I had the fastest vessel on the sea equipped with the best and most modern machinery. This vessel was built in Charleston and finished in Galveston, painted dark brown and christened the *Jupiter*.

Ambassador De Onis protested more loudly and thus forced President Monroe to send agents to Texas to verify the installation of the French refugees under the authority of General L'Allemand and warn him that he was on American territory. George Graham, a self-appointed official, was chosen for the investigation. Mr. Graham was involved in the bank business in Washington, and he was always ready for investments when the opportunity arose. Mr. Graham did not support Luis De Onis. Then Mr. De Onis protested to Secretary John Quincy Adams about the French invasion of Texas. Mr De Onis and Mr. Adams could not agree on their points of view. The matter, which concerned only Secretary Adams, was to prevent the Anglo-American invasion of Texas. Mr. Adams said little about my commune, but when he learned that my privateers were seizing British vessels, he protested along with the rest of the Cabinet.

Mr. Graham gave General L'Allemand permission to remain to colonize after some loan agreements. Mr. Graham did not know that General L'Allemand was under oath and had obligations to New Orleans.

The Indians were neglected, not considered, and left prey to war fever that the agitators and former English secret agents had previously fomented. France had been defeated under Napoleon and enjoyed little prestige or credit with Washington officials. Many French refugees were only tolerated and not readily accepted as immigrants when they wanted to colonize empty areas of the United States. It is not from vanity that I state with total frankness that if the French refugees had had the opportunity of being admitted as colonists in the United States after Napoleon's defeat, Indian revolts west of the Appalachians would have been fewer. All historians recognized the hard labor of the first French monks and the great efforts they made in exploring far ahead without exploiting the Indians, but by properly inculcating good morals in them.

There is no record of war between the French and the Indians. The wars between the English and the Indians are numerous and will remain so in the future. Strong liquor certainly did not contribute to calming or defeating the Indians.

Mr. Beverly Chew, the customs officer, was the most difficult man to get by at his post in New Orleans. He would never have known much about our captures of Spanish ships without the information furnished to him by Commodore D.C. Patterson, who kept watch with his fleet stationed at New Orleans. Beverly Chew always acted according to Patterson's orders. Patterson already knew what kind of spoils we were taking from the Spanish vessels, and he also knew that we were receiving secret help from some officers of the American Army and other great men like Jn R. Grymes, E. J. Livingston, Jn Blanque, and many others. When one of our vessels could not get by the post of Beverly Chew at New Orleans with customs duties to pay, then we would try other vessels with other captains. They passed without difficulty.

During my stay in New Orleans and other cities, some of my officers exercised poor judgment with the vessels that they had been assigned in Galveston. Captain Mitchell went beyond all rules and orders in trying to construct a storehouse in Barataria with the goal of starting legal operations for the entry of merchandise into Louisiana. Commodore Patterson, stationed at New Orleans, made an incursion against Captain Mitchell's vessels and destroyed the new storehouse; certain objects were sold by D.C. Patterson for his personal use. Commodore Patterson began to give chase to some of my seized vessels, but he never ventured too far out on the high seas.

English vessels captured by my privateer captains and recaptured by Commodore Patterson were sold at auction. Part of the money reverted to its owners, part to the American treasury, and part to Commodore Patterson and his subordinates. My vessel *Carmelita* did good business between Mobile, New Orleans, and Galveston. We declared false destinations at New Orleans, for I intended to smuggle the merchandise into other ports.

The largest and fastest of my steamships, the *Jupiter*, did the same, and like all the others escaped custom duties at New Orleans. We would transport construction material for houses and hide cannon powder on board in every other wine barrel. On board the *Jupiter* also, one barrel out of every two was empty so as to place silk or other precious materials that could be smuggled in it, or even bronze or wrought iron objects for other Atlantic ports.

For secret commercial agent in New Orleans, I had Mr. De Ariza: he also had the responsibility of preparing for the secret occupation of Florida. I conveyed vessels to Arsène Latour, one of my best technicians. On April 18, 1817, I left Campeche on the *Devrador*. I arrived in New Orleans on April 28 and relieved Uncle Reyné of the *Rita* and the *Industria*, which he had captured before I established the Campeche commune. I had the *Rita* fitted at the same time as the *Intrepido,* which under the name of *New Enterprise,* was sold to Antoine Bonafacio.

My brother Pierre did not spend much time with his family. His eldest son never cared about being around him; his third son lived in Galveston for some time and then returned to his home on the banks of the Sabine.

During our stay in Washington we made some trips to Philadelphia to see my sister Yvonne and my father. My father died at the age of 74 before my return to Galveston. My brother Pierre spent a few weeks with my sister Yvonne. She was two years and five months older than Pierre and my elder by five years. My brother Pierre began to detach himself from the family. His eldest son, Pierre, remained in New Orleans while another of his sons, Eugène, accompanied us. His other son, Cézar, lived with his mother and sisters near the Sabine River. Pierre was an active businessman; his mind knew no rest. He was two and a half years my elder. Some time later his family went to settle near New Orleans and a little farther up the Sabine River.

My brother Alexandre was not in good health after those summer months of 1816 and due to serious injuries that he sustained when the vessel *Sinue Que Non* capsized near the Mexican coast on

April 7, 1814. Most of his crew perished—— both from the mistreatment he received during his arrest in September 1814, as well as from the constant operating of his batteries, from the dangers of the battles of New Orleans.

My brother Alexandre was ll years older than I, was shorter, and weighed more than I; but his physical condition was no longer as good as it had been until the date of his last sea voyage to the rescue of Napoleon in the early spring of 1815. My brother Alexandre rendered precious secret services to New Orleans; he was well known because of his skill as the best cannoneer, killing all the British officers and their horses.

Uncle Reyné, "The Valiant," was also an adroit artilleryman in the batteries. He was 12 years older than my brother Alexandre. Uncle Reyné was in good health and rendered very good secret service to Joseph Bonaparte. Uncle Reyné commanded vessels in Venezuela and worked secretly with Generals L'Allemand and De Aury.

My brother Pierre and I worked hard and fast, and we captured the Spanish vessels that were returning loaded in the port of Campeche each week. Angelo Benito De Ariza was named secretary of the Consul, Mr. Castillon, in New Orleans with the salary of 100 dollars per month, which he received from Havana.

My brother Alexandre had taken the false name of General, either Jontelle or Johnson or Jossonet. No one ever discovered his real name. He also used the name of Youx and later received the sobriquet of Dominique Youx. My brother Alexandre died on November 14, 1830. He presently lies in the New Orleans cemetery, and on his tomb inscribed with the name of Dominique-You, after a long, elegiac passage, is a Masonic emblem of the charitable society of which he was a member. My brother Alexandre died at the age of 59.

Pierre and I entrusted two vessels to General Claussel. As he could not enter Philadelphia with the French refugees, we loaded extra food and provisions on board his ships and gave him the order to enter at Vera Cruz. Great diversions took place in Washington and other cities, Philadelphia, Baltimore, and Charleston, while I was very busy ordering my affairs concerning the construction of my commune in Galveston. My Galveston commune began to wonder if it were necessary to accept other French refugees.

My brother Pierre was deceived by Mr. Picornell, who sent him false reports, which caused disagreement and ended the good relations which had prevailed between them. Father De Sedella sent a total sum of 19,900 dollars to my brother Pierre. Pierre acquitted himself and paid 6,000 dollars more than was needed, as the audit of accounts proved later.

The secretary responsible then was Felipe Fatio, who was old and in poor health. The priest De Sedella advised him to retire. He replaced him with Manuel García in February 1819 or there about. Felipe Fatio was to die on February 4, 1820. He was of the Latin race and born in Switzerland 69 years earlier. Letters exchanged between him and his officers disappeared, which caused problems. Manuel García replaced Felipe Fatio in February 1819.

During the winters of 1817 and 1818 our prizes, in Negroes as in merchandise, coming from Cuba and the high sea poured into the port of my commune and took on agreeable proportions. Many of those Negroes were sold to planters and businessmen come from as far away as Saint Louis. The Bowie brothers were the biggest buyers of Negroes. Jn and Christophe Lisa bought a large number of Negroes headed for Saint Louis in the state of Missouri, in exchange for worked leather articles and shoes from Saint Louis.

Mr. Lucien Fontenelle brought me a letter from Saint Louis. He was a commercial agent with the Indians. I also received a friendly letter from Mr. Joseph Robidoux, who lived in Saint Joseph. I had the most business with Manuel Lisa of Saint Louis . Mr. Gratiot also made purchases as did Mr. Papin and others.

The Negro slaves sent to Saint Louis at the same time as the merchandise were exchanged for silver coins. Back then, I counted many partisans of high morality, imbued with humanitarian feelings, and many sympathizers among the businessmen of different cities of the Atlantic coast and in the interior. Mr. Wade Hampton wrote me many letters for orders of slaves for some time——up to 4,019 slaves by sea to Charleston.

While I was on mission to Washington and in the three other cities of Baltimore, Philadelphia, and New York, I formed the plan of going to Boston to do business with Mr. Bostwick, and then go to Charleston to make a business visit to Mr. Mortimore. I then wanted to visit the family of Mr. Wade Hampton at Tygre River in the northwest of the state of South Carolina. I then wanted to visit the family of Mr. George Allen at Mobile and to Grande Isle to visit with Mr. François Rigaud. I then wished to visit the family of Mr. Arsène Lebleu in the Bayou of Calcasieu.

I received numerous letters from distinguished explorers who were active in the Missouri Territory and the northern zone of Louisiana. I intended equally to accompany the Bowie brothers and go up the Mississippi with them and visit Memphis, Saint Louis, and other fur markets farther north.

General Wilkinson heartily complimented those men and advised me to invest more in the North. I kept up important business relations with them through my agents in New Orleans and Alexandria. It is with Dumay Saint Martin of Donaldsonville that I dealt with most in business. Mr. Martin had shares in four vessels. He received the tenth part of prizes on land and a fifth from sea prizes as insurance policy underwriter.

The plan of action adopted by us at that time in New Orleans included the confiscation of the goods of rich exploiters by our privateering vessels under the authority of our letters of marque and then the distribution of those riches to those in need in the majority class. We ran into many obstacles even within our own organization with a small number of officers as well as from the owners of private banks and politicians in Washington

However, despite this opposition and the damage inflicted upon my commune at Grande Terre, I continued to bring my material aid to the army of the United States in New Orleans so as to save the Union from the British invasion, and I remained faithful to my convictions, becoming even more decided than ever to fulfill the mission I had given myself by establishing a good government based upon liberty, truth and justice, and equality for all and the elimination of special privileges.

Jn Laffite

Carlinville, Monday, November 9, 1846

Our meetings in New Orleans always had constant changes as was indicated earlier, and eventually they became well known through the intermediary of certain of our members captured by the Spanish, who forced confessions to find out our secrets in regard to the marque commission.

While the officials were detained in Washington by the negotiations of their treaties, they investigated the problem of French refugees. They were unaware of the exact landing site because those parts of the Texas coast were neither in United States territory nor under their surveillance at that time. My captains brought me rich quantities of silver, gold, Negro slaves, and merchandise of all kinds.

My captains had to fight intense battles on the high sea. Some of them disappeared with their cargo; they were the kind not to share their prizes and preferred disappearing rather than paying a tax to the commune. William Mitchell tried to do the same; he kept patents made out in my name. He set about establishing his own commune in Barataria. Thanks to his gold he easily succeeded among the merchants of New Orleans. D.C. Patterson soon discovered his weak point and confiscated all his properties.

Again my name was put before the public, accused of having approved a privateer base on United States territory. The unreasonable conduct of those officers on land and on the sea caused some of my secret plans to be divulged to Spain and Washington. We ran into the open opposition of the Spanish ambassador, De Onis, who raised protests to President Monroe and Secretary John

Adams. We also encountered a certain resistance in Haiti among the lethargic black officials working at Port-au-Prince.

Our final meeting of last resort finished badly in the presence of the priest De Sedella. Our assembly ended with the dismissal of several officers, from which General Mina, Henry Perry, General Soto De Marina, Raymon Espagnol, General De Aury, and General L'Allemand were excluded, for they had refrained from attending and were inclined to abuse alcoholic drinks and violate discipline, let themselves be corrupted, furnished information to Spanish royalists, and thus made themselves the authors of their own weakness and eventual defeats.

My vessels were searched many times: certain vessels were prevented from transporting merchandise, slaves, gold, silver, and cannons and powder when it was discovered that they belonged to me, forcing me to find other methods.

I only felt a moderate fear in regard to Spain, against which its American provinces had rebelled: but I strongly feared the Washington officials, for they were on good terms with England. Those officials easily accepted the signature of compromise treaties, allowing their country to gather enough strength in any way and under any form, to build up a treasury to support an expansion based upon loans from private commercial enterprises. Their attitude was completely different from my program of government and contrary to the Declaration of Independence, that sacred document which I have highly venerated to this very day, to which I, one day, sacrificed almost all that I possessed because I wanted to spare it from being trampled. In those days, Washington officials were laboriously working to rebuild the nation.

Not daring to spread forth that sacred document before the world, they lost their footing and renounced the true principles of the great American and French Revolutions, based on life, liberty, and the pursuit of happiness. Until the very present I have been a witness to the negligence with which the official powers have treated that sacred manuscript.

On March 2, 1818, John Whitman was hanged in New Orleans for having struck down an officer of the Confederated Army in 1813. His trial dragged on until, finally, he could not absolve himself of firing first. His attorneys cost me 9,000 dollars. The execution of John Whitman gave the papers the chance to widely publish false news about my commune.

The activities of my privateers against Spanish vessels continued to cause protests in Washington. I was powerful at sea but defenseless on land. Later I was to realize that De Onis was keeping an access to Texas for himself through his protests which reached Washington, Madrid, and even London.

In New Orleans, as in Washington, everyone began to believe that I had been defeated at sea. I was all-powerful on the ocean but in a state of inferiority on land, not having sufficient land forces. This situation furnished traffickers the opportunity to infiltrate Louisiana through the north and to those self-styled representatives of Washington, Havana, and Mexico to dictate certain terms to me. I notified them all that I would not accept pulling back and replied to them that always having adhered to the principles of the first French Revolution, I would never change.

Armed gangs, certain ones led by Englishmen who claimed that they were American pioneers, began to penetrate through the north. Certain of my officers were discovered in the act of smuggling with those armed bands and found themselves with the following alternative: a trial in court or a duel with me. I was 36 at the time my Campeche commune began to prosper before the storm. I was an expert duelist and none could handle a sword as well as I.

The British government kept secret agents in all the ports of America to spy on me, but without success. Spain also had its secret service officers: mediocre illiterates in the business of espionage research. They were fine swordsmen though none of them equaled my dueling skill. I went to Baltimore to visit Louis Brion, who was a secret agent for my business concerning commerce with South America in Baltimore. I got in contact with two British officials who claimed to be American businessmen. In face of their provocative behavior I was forced to fight them in a duel. They both met their end and were never spoken of again.

My officers disguised themselves, as did I, during our appearance or presence in strange places. Information always reached me through English secret service officers who claimed to be sailors, under the pretext of jumping their ships, to gather information about business in the interior or about internal conditions of the cities along the sea coast. I encountered a fair number of them; first to string them along, next to take them off to a deserted location. They never saw England again. Many incidents occurred. Thanks to a careful search of their baggage, they were uncovered and eliminated. If they had no proof of their identity, we extracted a confession from them after amusements or good hospitality. What a man hides in himself comes to light after too much fun intoxicates him. I discovered that the English government had never sent officers to agitate or stay in the city of Boston or that of Washington.

Mr. Bonaparte had some officers who spied and did police research and recruitment of British officers. They came to New York but did not stay long; they left toward the west, to Ohio or toward Philadelphia and Baltimore.

At that time I was completely busy; it was hardly easy to create communes and to set them up to endure. That vast new country lent itself to every kind of commercial expansion and allowed a few rare privileged people to pose as pioneers while disregarding the laws that ordered the creation of schools of higher education open to all the emigrants from the backward nations of Europe.

At that time I was struggling with all my energy and would doubtless have succeeded in reducing Spain's power to a minimum while also improving the future condition of the inhabitants of Texas and the Far West. I was up against strong opposition and ran into numerous obstacles caused by acts of my own officers and due also to the indifference prevailing in Washington. That opposition was also attributable to the fact that I had not formed a constitutional assembly or established a solid defense system on land as I had on the high sea. The majority of my officers were agnostics, but the English speaking officers were Protestants. Harmony reigned among them; religious quarrels were unknown to them.

Father De Sedella did not know my secret codes, but around October 1818, he learned that certain of my secrets were being divulged. It is why Felipe Fatio, before departing, revealed a part of my secrets to Picornell and some staff officers, saying that the so-called agnostic French refugees who were invading the east of Texas did not have any holy religion and Inquisition of Father Antonio De Sedella [sic].

The priest De Sedella never had the least idea that I was using him to obtain money from the governor of Havana under false pretenses. From the start, at the time of our first meetings during the course of the year 1814, I realized that Father De Sedella was one of those men who act under cover and behind a mask, passing himself off as a tender-hearted being, stupid enough to turn his pockets inside out and empty them. He revealed himself, along with the plans of the Spanish government, in the hope that I would gradually lose confidence and all patriotism toward the government of the United States from the fact that the latter refused to give me back my property or give me compensation of any kind at all for the help that I had given when it was a question of saving the United States from complete destruction.

The priest De Sedella gave me his assent on numerous matters so as to obtain some of my officers, but we were not able to agree on the question of recruiting men from the American New England, that is to say, the states of Massachusetts, Rhode Island, Connecticut, and the state of Maryland, for he claimed that they were not familiar with the customs of Latin America. He also refused the recruitment of Americans native to the states of Virginia, Kentucky, and Tennessee. In fact, he refused his agreement for the recruiting of Americans living in the North and South of the United States. First of all, he wanted me to give up my privateering commission and to accept the colonial statute of the Spaniards. In the second place, he asked to grant to a religious denomination the privilege of establishing itself in the provinces and the principal territorial subdivisions.

I realized in the third place that he had no respect for the Declaration of Independence or for the constitutional laws of the United States. In fourth place, I realized that by ingenious strata- gems he had no other goal but to favor the return of all the Loui- siana Territory to Spain. Fifthly, I realized that all his subterfuges differed in nothing from the practices employed by his Church to hinder the development of all forms of good, liberal government. In the sixth place, I was convinced that he used the name of inde- pendence only to render possible the establishment of a powerful religious syndicate with the goal of hindering all progress or devel- opment of liberal thought.

I also realized that he was for independence in name only, and in reality he wished nothing better than to see that word com- pletely forgotten within the dictionary. I realized too that he had no talent for abetting progress and that the application of the methods he recommended could have no other result than the masses' progressive impoverishment. His methods differed widely from mine and the projects I had inherited from my good grand- mother to continue the struggle against the restrictive laws of the governments which used the Church to gain headway by force of arms or any other method in order to subjugate peoples and re- turn to the past. My grandmother taught me never to compro- mise nor let myself be influenced by the offer of gold or silver to slacken the march of progress.

He [De Sedella] took up the habit of dressing up in symbols of independence, but in reality he had neither the inventive talent nor the initiative necessary for progress. He still adhered to the principles of those around him and worked for the establishment of the clergy in a powerful syndicate that would definitively de- stroy its own laws by impoverishing the popular masses.

The first revolt will take place in 1859 and 1909, then, or at a certain period, the clergy conducted an Inquisition whose results did nothing for the liberation of the lower people [sic]. Britain, cuttlefish and octopus, will begin to lose its tentacles in 1912; it will have lost them all 80 years later. A state should be governed as one cooks a small fish: carefully. Whoever wishes to take over the world to change its form will lose it. Whoever will try to reform it will lose it: whoever will aid an oppressor with force will lose it by force. The first emperors will be dethroned during the year 1910. In Europe the second group of emperors will lose their thrones in 1919.

Jn Laffite

Sangamon, Tuesday, December 1, 1846

Before the hurricane everything was going perfectly, and the commune was prospering despite the protests from the Spaniards. Rumors were spread concerning the storm and the damage that it had caused. Mr. Noël arrived from New Orleans, named to the position of General Director of the commune. After the storm of September 1818 the new founding of Galveston and the numerous arrangements to rebuild my city caused me greater and grave problems.

New laws were passed. New courts of law were established. Crimes like piracy, murder, theft, and mutiny were punishable by hanging. The courts were comprised of a jury of 13 members and three judges. Two of my old vessels were transformed into offices after the storm. The *Ciel Bleu* and the *Saragosa* were their names. The *Saragosa* was transformed into a customs office for the examination of the goods of the privateer captains.

One of my forts situated 21 kilometers from the Trinity River was destroyed. I had the damage repaired by four carpenters, five masons, and two blacksmiths. This fort was 45 kilometers from Galveston. Everything went well, but not as well as before the storm had ravaged the commune.

Spain was increasing its business and commercial exchanges

with the United States and some other countries of Europe, spending large sums of money to convince the United States to abolish privateer commissions. John De Laporte and Herman Grammaton were at work in Galveston and honest at their work but too generous in awarding letters of marque. Pierre La Maison operated along Venezuela's coast up to the Yucatan. He brought back large loads of merchandise.

Governor Cagigos made me payments while I was in Philadelphia; the funding rose to 15,000 dollars. I received the last sum from the governor on April 30, 1819. It was a goodly sum of 12,000 dollars, just in time before I was discovered as an enemy double agent and traitor to Spain.

Two captured vessels were sold in Baltimore. The operation's profit was shared among Pierre and me, David De Forrest, Mr. Garrot, Louis Brion, Mr. Guestier, Mr. Maire, Mr. Livingston, Mr. Grymes: all received two percent shares in gold.

I neglected my own interests to form a new constitution. I had put my confidence in several Washington officials. I made the error of showing generosity in my interior affairs. The hurricane that destroyed my commune of Campeche caused the beginning of a reactionary movement and furnished traffickers the opportunity to demoralize my commune and buy certain of my officers and cause them to abandon their principles concerning support of freedom.

I was full of courage and force of will despite the many obstacles that alleged representatives of a country, with ill-disguised characters and their own agendas and who claimed nonexistent titles, set up against the future of my communes and tried to exercise a discouraging effect on my communes.

The Carancahua Indians brought us important help in exchange for which I gave them cooking utensils, knives, powder, and some small muskets. Later, after having been well treated and paid, they pilfered a quantity of our provisions. It took a month to repair a small part of the damage caused by the hurricane. We left the most important damages for later.

George Graham, a banker and venal politician in Washington, arrived in Galveston a month before the hurricane. President Monroe had given him an order to study the justice system and the government that existed in my commune. He claimed himself to be an official envoy. I treated him with the greatest courtesy and received him with the best hospitality in the world. He stayed with me for two weeks. He was of an agreeable nature, and every day we would hunt and fish together. He could not understand why I was giving equal rights to everyone without consideration of nationality or religion. He represented exactly the same type as Alexander Hamilton and opposed Thomas Jefferson's principles. I knew he was a treacherous liar and dissimulator. He was in the business of banking and loans and was ready to lend money at a very high interest rate to the first colonist leader who came along: he tried to upset my system of government and met with Mr. L'Allemand, in charge of French colonization.

George Graham left us on September 9, 1818, and stopped in New Orleans and different ports before reaching Washington again. He described the weakness of my army to all the officers of the army and navy and reported that my system of government was weak and worn out and offered no opportunities to lazy intellectuals. He let it be understood that this form of government on the frontiers represented a danger and stated that I must be sent to some province in South America. Mr. Graham told me that the territory located beyond the Sabine River to the west of the Rio Grande belonged to the United States, which did not authorize me to establish a commune of my choice west of that river.

Mr. Graham did not succeed in exercising his influence on my commune, but he made false allegations upon his return. Some of my officers were called to Washington to verify his statements. I received a notice coming from the Hotel Butler in Washington telling me to come answer the accusations of Mr. Graham. My brother Pierre, several officers, and I left for Washington to examine the reports of Mr. Graham.

Mr. Garrot was our chief representative in Washington and

Philadelphia. We arrived in Washington in mid November, 1818. I immediately went to find Secretary Adams. He was about 51 then, and I was 36. He received and treated me with great consideration. He stated that he had never authorized Mr. Graham to investigate Galveston. According to him, Mr. Graham was working for himself. As to the order to depart, it came from Mr. Graham alone and not from an official of the United States government. Mr. Adams maintained that Mr. Graham was in the banking business and was interested above all in loans and credit to private enterprises, and that he liked neither the ideas of Thomas Jefferson nor the systems of Napoleon.

With me in Washington I had François Little, who left for Baltimore in November 1818. He had the rank of a captain on my vessels when he retired in 1822. He became a furniture manufacturer. Mr. Ely Ramsey was also a great friend from Baltimore. His two sons often came to visit me, even in Galveston.

Information still came to me from English secret service officers claiming to be sailors. I made a report to Secretary Adams in Washington concerning their secret work of subversion, saying that they had maps and intentions of stirring up the Indians farther to the west. The government increased its secret scouting missions toward the West. Some were directed toward the South and the Cherokee Indian tribes in North and South Carolina and Tennessee.

I failed in my mission to Washington. Upon my return to New Orleans, then to Galveston, my mission to Washington over, I found that my officers were violating some of the commune's laws; I found new faces there, recently recruited to my commune. A revision was initiated to establish a new court for the lawbreakers and the guilty.

James Campbell, John McHenry, William Cochrane, Theodore Rawlins, and Mr. Grammaton entered into service as principal personnel. John De Laporte was named secretary-in-chief of the commune's business. John Ducoing resigned at the same time as Ramon Vagnol (Spaniard) on January 1, 1818. Mr. De Rieux and

Mr. Lafton also resigned from their positions in New Orleans. John and Js Rousselin (two brothers) stayed for a while at the colony.

I realized that my commune was undergoing rapid changes; however, the secrets in New Orleans were no longer efficiently kept. The Spanish governor of Havana began to realize that all the while we received a large amount of money to help the Spanish royalists in Texas, we simultaneously damaged their lifelines on the ocean. I hated the Spanish Army more than any other. The course that others took to attempt to invade Texas by leaving from the Gulf coast was destined for failure. The system that I used and by which I held back their reserves at sea was weakening the Spanish Army in the interior. Returning to my commune in Galveston, I learned that the British spy system had left their operations base in Baltimore and Philadelphia for other ports toward the west, as well as toward the north, in the vicinity of their Canadian possession. General Wilkinson sent many good wishes to Manuel Lisa and heartily congratulated him on the excellence of the commercial relations between New Orleans and the extreme North.

Manuel Lisa's son, Christophe, visited me during the short time I stayed in Baltimore. He then went to Boston, and later came to live with me while I was on a mission to Washington in the year of grace 1818.

General Wilkinson greatly praised his men in Saint Louis and advised me to visit them. Recognition of the United States was rapidly increasing; more and more treaties were signed. But entirely despite my opposition, he was also giving others access to the northeast coast of Texas, opening a breach to men like Adair, Long, Johnson, Smith, and Bigelow, who had stolen——I am certain——a large portion of their provisions on board my river boats with the complicity of some new financiers like Graham, Ripley, Ross, Patterson, Oliver, and many others.

One of my vessels leaving for Saint Louis to Mr. Lisa and Mr. Hempstead never reached that city. It held Negro slaves, a large quantity of merchandise, food-stuffs, and hardware. My men had loaded it near Alexandria, Louisiana. It was seized close to Natchez; all the merchandise on board was sold off to third parties, and the group of slaves was led off with my captain, Hernan Ortiz. This vessel was captured on or aroune April 10, 1819. Captain Ortiz returned to Galveston in the following summer in June 1819. He wore different clothes, notably a cap and fur coat. He told me how his boat had been stolen from him above Natchez. He did not speak English well but had grasped some of the words from the mouths of the robbers of his boat. He stated that he heard those men give one of their group the title of General Adair and another that of General Long. He stated that the above-named men must have worried about the Bowie brothers, that the Bowie brothers had intentions upon Texas and they were members of my commune, and that it would be necessary, with bribes, to distance them from the province of Texas.

I kept silent and did not give full faith to the statements of Captain Ortiz. I had him given a position in Venezuela with my Uncle Reyné. Just two months after relieving him from his duty and his transfer to Venezuela, my commune learned the truth concerning the two men Ortiz had mentioned. Those two men, Adair and Long, were those who indirectly accepted the cargo stolen above Natchez in April 1819.

The newcomers, like James Campbell, William Hall, William Cochrane, J.S. Seleik, Reyle Lacassinier, John McHenry, Clemente Lellande, and Gregory Toeye were men with tested ideas. They placed before my very eyes the thefts and trickery of the so-called officers from Natchez.

The Sabine River was declared the United States border. The Sabine and two other small rivers, the Calcasieu and the Mermentau, were used to transport goods to Alexandria. Bolivar was the main depot under the supervision of Mr. Hall, Mr. James Campbell, Mr. John R. Jones, Mr. Wade Hampton, Mr. William Cochrane, Mr. John McHenry, Mr. Dumis Martin, Mr. Jn Sauvinet, and the Bowie brothers, his aides, as well as Mr. John Blanque. The Bowie brothers were in charge of the North up to

Saint Louis. Messrs. Chouteau, Lucas, Gratiot, Lisa, Papin received some slaves at Saint Louis, which later caused them difficulties at Natchez.

Mr. Seleik came to open a store and a hotel, and he was allowed to establish his agency at the place named Bolivar. Mr. Hall represented my portion of the goods at Bolivar; he was a good second-in-command to my projects. He gave me a lot of information and wise advice about the people of the North. His opinions and information in regard to Bigelow, Johnson, Smith, Long, and several others were not very favorable. Mr. Hall had known them for a long time and realized that they stole merchandise in the interior.

James Campbell became one of my best secret officers in early 1819. I was fond of him and had confidence in him, having long known him; he was from Baltimore and had been a good sailor on American warships in the struggle against England. Captain Campbell, like the majority of good Americans, cordially detested the landlubber robbers. He had no respect for D.C. Patterson and the others who stole and sold my goods. He kept me up-to-date on James Long's dishonest methods.

Mr. Lacassinier came from Canada with 256 French families to settle in Texas. Mr. Lacassinier was an upright, honest man, born to govern. I had chosen him as a coast watcher between the Sabine and Matagorda. Mr. John De Laporte was sometimes his assistant, but he had to resign because of a skin ailment that affected his face and shoulders. He left for New Orleans.

Between the months of November 1818 and February 1819, my commune had 476,000 dollars put away. My brother Pierre was active in Washington. He stayed there longer than I. His protests and mission had no effect.

During the months of July to December 1819, and the first seven months of 1820, Spain counted on convoys to protect it. It transported a good quantity of silver and gold ingots across the Atlantic.

A portion was projected for American loans. At the end of

May 1819, James Long, a self-styled general, led his band of men from Nagodoches. He proclaimed himself President of Texas, assisted by some carefully chosen men as advisors. He knew my commune to be an important base of operations. He sent me James Gaines to negotiate with my officers' council, but they rejected his suggestions. He also sent two aides, one after the other, Mr. Johnson and Mr. Smith, who wished to consult me directly about an alliance. I wrote to James Long and discretely made clear to him that my intention was to help the French element in that part of the country. Mr. Johnson and Mr. Smith returned to James Long with the lengthy letter I had written at the beginning of July 1819. I had thought my letter would deter James Long from Galveston, but, to the contrary, it encouraged him to proceed; he sent another member of his general staff, named Bigelow.

He was the man whom I wanted to see, for Mr. Johnson had described him, without knowing him as the man that Captain Ortiz had seen embark on his vessel at Natchez. Mr. Bigelow came directly to see me; I received him cordially to get him to talk about James Long and his adventuresome organization of an army. I kept him completely drunk every day, and he was recognized by some of my men as the head of a gang of robbers who had boarded the boat of Captain Ortiz at Natchez.

I held Bigelow in contempt, but I never showed my feelings and kept him as long as he wished to remain. I did not furnish him any information that could be useful to his leader, James Long. I wanted to capture this gang of robbers. I sent three men, Gregory Toeye, Clemente Lellande, and Ricardo Touzias, to General Pérez, a Spaniard, so that he might arrest those robbers who passed themselves off in Texas as good patriots. In June 1819 James Long had 5,000 men at Nagadoches. Fewer than 100 came out unhurt from the battle with General Pérez. He sent me a note telling me that he had killed only 152 of James Long's men. The majority deserted, and 107 wound up in Galveston.

General Pérez eliminated the majority of James Long's men. He and some of his officers arrived in Galveston; then he went to

New Orleans to enroll some men into his decimated army. He left Warren Hall, Mr. Smith, and some men at Galveston and Bolivar. Mr. Hall and Mr. Smith talked to me about James Long and his plans concerning his mercenary band.

James Long returned to Texas with a reinforced army and suffered a second defeat at the hands of the Spaniards commanded by General Pérez. James Long came to Galveston after his second defeat. I treated the majority of the other citizens well so as to get all the news out of him that I could. He admitted that Mr. Graham had promised him loans if he could conquer the larger part of Texas and use Galveston as a port of entry.

After his second defeat, Long joined Mr. D.C. Patterson, Mr. Ripley, and several others upon his return to New Orleans. He feared making another attack in Texas and discovered that Mr. Hall was responsible for the commerce between Bolivar and Galveston, which decided him to join the newspapers and Patterson's group in New Orleans.

Messrs. Hall, Cochrane, McHenry, and Mr. Campbell were new to my commune: all proved to be sincere and loyal.

At the time of the arrival of Mr. Smith and Mr. Johnson in Galveston, I bought a vessel in New Orleans, *Le Brave,* and awarded it and its crew of 20 men to Captain Desfarges and his assistant, Robert Johnston. All my captains had letters of marque that I myself had given them: with one, instructions; two, rules to open fire only to stop Spanish and English vessels; three, to take nothing from American vessels. At that time most American merchandise was transported on Spanish vessels, which troubled and confused some of my captains, who were hindered by finding American cargo under the Spanish flag, which is what De Onis and Graham and Spain heartily desired in order to have more power and protection.

Patterson and some other officers residing in New Orleans were on the lookout and formed a scheme to keep the vessel from going to sea. The *U.S.S. Alabama* was fairly far from the Mississippi's mouth, about two leagues from the south quay [sic]. Captain

Desfarges fired on a Spanish vessel, the *Filomena.* The *U.S.S. Alabama* drew near and also fired, which caused a certain amount of disorder. Captain Desfarges and his First Mate Robert Johnston ordered the crew to fire back and take over the Spanish vessel, *Filomena.* The *Alabama* fired some cannon shots and took over my vessel. The entire crew of *Le Brave* was taken off to New Orleans to be judged under the charge of piracy.

A crew member of *Le Brave* jumped off and escaped before the capture of the ship. He was Lancer Wooding. I did not see him again until March 1832 when I stopped in Philadelphia. He was an honest, sincere man who told me the full truth concerning the capture of *Le Brave.* We bid each other goodbye, and he promised me never to speak to anyone of my coming to Philadelphia. He married under another name.

Captain Desfarges and Robert Johnston were hanged in New Orleans on Friday morning, May 26, 1820. Two men were acquitted; the 13 others were kept for a long time in prison then executed almost a year later with four others who had stolen some slaves from planters. Mr. Grymes and Mr. Livingston were the attorneys of those men.

Crowds sympathetic to the crew of *Le Brave* gathered in the city; riots began in favor of Desfarges and Johnston, his lieutenant. This violence worsened the situation, for the authorities became intractable, maintaining their decisions, and showing themselves more and more ill-disposed toward the accused. The reasons that were given to my brother and me differed entirely from those the authorities gave. Their intention was to destroy our colony. We did not have a press to defend us. The *Courier de la Louisiane* was paid to print reports, and even those Creoles whom we had helped began to attack us.

The judgment took place at the end of 1819 and the start of 1820. My brother Pierre and I had written a request to the authorities with the aid of our attorneys, Mr. Livingston and John Grymes, but the judges turned a deaf ear, and the population continued to fatten on the flesh of the lamb.

George Brown, whom I had had executed at Galveston, confessed before he died that he had recruited men of James Long and General Adair for the robbery of Queue de Tortue Bayou in Saint Landry Parish on the night of September 25, 1819. All the men were of English origin except Brown, who was an Italian, and José de Guana, who was a Spaniard. Mr. John Lyons had owned his slaves for hardly a year when they were stolen from him. I had given almost all of them to him after the hurricane; most were women; all were injured by the storm and could not be sold. One old slave woman was badly injured, and I gave him a young 20-year-old woman also.

After the hurricane several planters came to buy cheaply or obtain for free the slaves that I furnished them out of generosity to help out the commune. Many thieves heard about the generosity I had shown the planters and found it easy to steal those slaves from their owners whom I had helped after the September 1818 storm. I gladly helped Lieutenant Js McIntosh seize those men. Two of the men taken to New Orleans were found innocent, and I learned that George Brown had forced them to take part in the robbery under the threat of death.

Jealousy arose in some of my captains, and naturally cupidity took hold of some, which caused them to upset things, to rob and pillage the weak, defenseless planters. Many of the Negro slaves and much gold jewelry that I had given my friends near the Calcasieu and Mermentau rivers were stolen by some of my men who had kicked up their heels. George Brown, an Italian whose real name was Ratti, became the leader of that gang of plantation robbers. Brown has been named as an assistant to Mr. Lacassinier at 100 dollars a month to help prepare the territories for the French Canadian colonists. George Brown abandoned Mr. Lacassinier at the quay [sic] of Calcasieu Bayou. He used a small sailboat to carry the Negroes stolen from the planters and then tried to sell them elsewhere inland. George Brown and José de Guana had done the same thing before the arrival of Lacassinier. The American Coast Guard pursued Brown and his boat, but he escaped with his 16

men and walked most of the way to Bolivar. Four of the men captured by the vessel *Lynx* of the United States had formerly been
with James Long. Warren Hall and William Cochrane reported to
me on their underhanded methods.

Mr. Lacassinier thought that Brown wandered in the interior
under the pretext of preparing land for the French Canadian colonists. George Brown and his 16 men were arrested by my officers,
brought to justice, found guilty, and condemned to be hanged tall
and high. And, naturally, the newspapers of New Orleans took
advantage of it to create scandalous publicity against my communes.

My brother Pierre wrote to Commodore Patterson on January
3, 1820, filing a claim in the name of the commune, and request-
ing a response; he received the order of having to evacuate Galveston.
Our prestige was evaporating in New Orleans; courts of law no
longer aided us, for Patterson, Oliver, Ripley, Graham, and De
Onis had more influence there than anybody. Those young shady
merchants, who had begun their businesses thanks to loans thatthe
bank had granted them, held Spain in high regard.

The nation was still young and recruited just about anyone to
press its business onward toward the west: the future was clearly
revealed by the development that the railroads began to take 12
years after I left Galveston. It was the beginning of steamboats.
The newspapers reached a greater number of readers. All this began to strangle my government. . . I had many businessmen in
New Orleans and many planters who supported the defense against
Spain by *Le Brave*, but as I said above, they were too busy with the
progress of the new nation and had almost forgotten both its birth
and its savior. My brother Pierre wrote to Havana on Jan. 7, 1820,
revealing James Long's conduct, but his letter had no effect.

Despite all those hurdles I continued my march forward. On
November 10, 1820, I entrusted a vessel to James Campbell and
John Marotte on another small ship that was to sail with him from
south Mexico along the north coast of South America.

Captain Campbell realized that a part of his cargo was missing, and he had Marotte called up for an explanation. John Marotte denied having kept any silver or bars of gold after handing over the Negroes of the commune. He falsely stated that the gold and silver had fallen overboard. I asked where they were hidden. John Marotte remained on the defensive and challenged me to a duel. As was the custom, each one drank a cup of coffee on the dueling field, then John Marotte collapsed, pleaded for his life, and admitted to where he had hidden the gold and silver. I slapped him and sent him off to the officers of the colony. He was ordered to leave within 24 hours with nine others of his ilk.

It was Friday, December 22, 1820, that Marotte and his henchmen were sent away from the commune. Ten days later a messenger arrived to inform me that John Marotte and seven of his men wanted to assassinate me, along with some of my officers, on board the *Saragosa* on the eve of January first, 1821. That day, Mr. Hall, Mr. Rigaud, Mr. Orozco, Mr. Campbell, Mr. Cochrane, and I stood watch in the cabin next to the strongboxes on the *Saragosa*. We heard nothing. James Campbell and François Rigaud and Philippe Orozco stayed awake. They heard footsteps approach and the cabin door creak. James Campbell fired the first shot at Marotte. We all woke and fired at the seven others. The next day we threw them overboard.

A great deal of turmoil arose within my commune, where the majority of the ordinary members did not know how to read or write. I did not have a single propaganda newspaper at my disposal to clarify to my commune the effects of the pressure exerted by Graham, Patterson, Oliver, Ripley, and the financiers of the United States who opposed the government of my commune. Those individuals, full of skill and tricks, worked out all sorts of plans to bring about discord, misunderstanding, and disorder among my officers. They began to make progress from the time the banker Graham caused the prestige, the influence, and the power of the United States to grow. They knew my commune was weakened and put in an awkward position by the hurricane. They knew the mass of the people were not interested in the sure, proven principles of the American Revolution or, above all, in that sacred manuscript document, the Declaration of Independence, to which at a given time my brothers Pierre and Alexandre and I had sacrificed almost all that we possessed at New Orleans.

They knew that I had greatly damaged Spanish commerce, thus leaving a free field to their selfish designs. They knew that I held supremacy on the sea, but that they had land forces in their favor. I lacked any. They knew the confidence of Europe, but they did not know what the aftereffect of internal struggles and revolutions is; they did not know the aftereffect of wars between nations. They did not know what they sowed would cause the beginning of a series of panics, wars, and epidemics. They did not know that the success of a single individual would later bring on the failure of 100 others. They cared little about the general interest and hardly thought about a panic like the one we witnessed in 1837. They did not imagine a corrupt political process like the one still in effect today; and, assuredly, they never reflected before acting.

Many men are blind; they are only children with hair on their chin. By engraving on silver coins the sacred inscription "in God we trust," they caused the most illiterate citizens to adore money and forget human laws and, above all, the spiritual commandments of divine providence that God had inculcated into the great men of the past.

In a near future, humanity will be engulfed and strangled in the coils of the British dragon; millions of beings will perish; and still other millions will find death in the epidemic that will follow.

My attitude toward that question has always been the following: How can man love God, whom he has never seen, when he does not love his brothers who are without cease before his eyes? I am not extremely religious. I have been present at many things in the past, and even today I feel no respect in regard to the British and Spanish dragons or to that of those hypocritical, dissimulating agents of corruption.

José Gasparilla was killed by his own men on November 15, 1820. He had been a brigand on the sea, pillaged American vessels, and all the blame landed on Pierre and me. José Gasparilla had worked on his own since the Battle of New Orleans. I had one of his captains executed for brigandage on an American vessel in Florida. His name was Francis Neely and had been paid off many times by Gasparilla to attack American vessels.

I still had a little hope in the few honest people of Galveston. My requests to the authorities were useless; my colony was shrinking; my courts proved to be without any value in the eyes of Washington.

Messrs. Graham, Johnson, Oliver, Davis were sent from New Orleans by the United States government to examine my form of government. They made an unfavorable report on my commune. We informed Mr. Graham that our government was against Spain and England and we would only abandon under the condition that the United States would occupy the Antilles and Florida. Mr. Graham was much more interested in the loans to make to Spain than in annexations of territory.

The principle that everything belonged to everyone, or in other terms, equality before all and the abolition of privileges of wealth, no longer gave such harmonious results. My brother Pierre and I had never thought that those for whom we had done so much at the time of the birth of a new nation would want to oust us from a foreign territory. Texas was not American territory; it still belonged to Spain, and it seemed that it was paying a foreign nation well to protect its territories and sea commerce. I had always rather worried about an invasion from Spain rather than an abandonment and destruction on the part of Washington.

Mr. De Onis did not keep his promise concerning the exchange of prisoners. My second meeting with him took place during my third mission to Washington in the presence of Secretary Adams and President Monroe. The Spanish government had about 110 of my men in Havana prison. I had 298 of their subjects in my prisons ready to be exchanged, including two monks and a bishop whom my officers had captured and relieved of their gold jewels. During my interviews Mr. De Onis always entered into crazy rages in regard to the three members of the clergy, a bishop and two priests, whom I was keeping in my prisons with an eye on a prisoner exchange.

The population of my colony was shrinking. Several men requested their payment in gold so as to become privateers on their own. Privateering commissions no longer existed. I began to make arrangements with the men and their families, furnishing them with small vessels to go where they wished.

Although the commune was ending, I kept my calm and was ready to help those who needed it. Several vigorous men were with me to maintain order.

Jean Laffite

EXILE FROM GALVESTON
AND A NEW LIFE

At Saint Genevieve, Monday, January 4, 1847

On Sunday, January 7, 1821, a warship appeared near the port. It was almost sunset. My officers and I thought that it was a Spanish warship. Captain Campbell left in a dinghy to verify its nationality and returned saying that it was the United States warship the *Enterprise,*

Early Monday morning I sent Captain Campbell with two other men in a small boat to escort the officers to port. Lieutenant Kearney disembarked; I shook his hand; he was very cordial and pleasant and complimented me on the means that I had employed to combat adversity. He revealed his sorrow when he read the message from the American government enjoining me to leave Galveston.

I saluted and bowed my head as a sign of respect for the order as soon as it appeared and showed no resentment for the two weeks that Lieutenant Kearney's visit lasted. After the agreeable stay of the Lieutenant and his men, I promised to be ready to leave Galveston seven weeks later. Lieutenant Kearney went back to sea with a promise to return at the time set.

I accepted with joy the ultimatum of the United States to have to leave Galveston.

Js Long, Patterson, and some others from New Orleans intended to gather some merchandise together for an auction sale to their benefit after I had left Galveston. I started to empty all my good buildings and gather up the materials, furniture, and anything that had some value. I divided all that: old furniture, jewels, food, and the vessels among all the members of the commune, telling them to leave, for I did not intend to leave anything behind to those New Orleans merchants.

The seven weeks were required to empty everything and share it among those who wanted to return to New Orleans or elsewhere. Most families headed toward the north or the banks of the Sabine. Some families were ready to embark with me.

Most of the work was finished on Saturday, February 24, 1821. On Sunday the twenty-fifth I suggested that all those who remained decorate the tombs of those who had died in the struggle against the Carancahua Indians three years before. My proposal was accepted to reduce two gold bars to a powder and spread it on the tombs. We spent two hours that beautiful Sunday taking a last walk on the west path of my commune.

Mr. Hall was my most trusted man. I left him all that I possessed of any value. I gave instructions to Mr. Hall and some men from Bolivar not to continue the Texas revolution until the moment was propitious. I let them know the Bowie brothers knew the topography of Texas better than Js Long and his companions.

I was more interested in Cuba than Texas. Cuba was the Spanish reserve base for the suppression of the Mexican provinces. Florida was acquired from Spain by the United States in 1819.

That Sunday, the twenty-fifth will always remain in my memory; my people made a last festival day of it, a last demonstration of gratitude before the dispersal of the colony. This colony had been founded to perpetuate a good government, firmly established by laws that prevented any individual being put on a pedestal, which assured equality to everyone and gave privileges to no one. Everyone regretted the disappearance of this egalitarian empire, to whose formation I had dedicated four years. The work was finished the following day; the men left with their families in different directions. They were to continue to organize the mild and the humble.

William Cochrane arrived with the news of the return of Lieutenant Kearney. I recommended to Mr. Hall, Mr. Campbell, Mr. Sherman, and those of Bolivar to keep our promise and distribute the gold to the indicated places. My last secret words to Mr. Hall were to say that my mission would be to the south, to the east, then to the north. The majority of my personal valuables and my documents had been sent to Charleston, Baltimore, and Philadelphia.

Lieutenant Kearney arrived on Thursday, March 1, 1821. He was deeply moved by the situation; he verified that the colony had dispersed and evacuated. I invited Lieutenant Kearney and all the crew on board my vessel to dine. As it was the last time he was to see Galveston——for we were not permitted to stay for more than 48 hours, I suggested that we make a tour of the commune to see what remained. We visited the tombs of those who had died in the war against the Indians. The tombs of the good-for-nothings executed on the orders of my courts were a sufficient proof that no pirate had ever been approved of or protected by me.

On March 3, 1821, I welcomed Lieutenant Kearney and his crew for one last time, and I bid my adieu to everyone. I was asked several questions to which I replied briefly. Preparations were made to set off the powder. I made a short speech in honor of those officers from Washington, praising their efforts to continue the Declaration of Independence.

Js Long was there, and he asked me if I would leave behind any of my materials. I replied curtly that Galveston would be burned. Everyone left the island at four o'clock. The sky cleared, and a breeze blew from the northwest. Fires were lit everywhere; the flames rose along the shoreline. My vessels set off toward the south. Four leagues to sea I could still see Galveston on fire like a sunset. That is the last time I saw the Texas Gulf.

My brother Pierre left New Orleans in mid February 1821. He feared being arrested after receiving a warning. He left for Savannah and Charleston. He left Charleston around the middle of April.

My four vessels arrived in the Yucatan on March 9, 1821. The merchandise coming from the Isla de Mujeres was discharged onto a small boat. Fresh food was brought to Dzilam. We departed from the Isla de Mujeres on March 21, 1821, for Venezuela, where I met my son Antoine. We remained in Cartagena until June 1821. Venezuela had declared its independence in 1819.

My brother Pierre and I met up in Cartagena in the middle of June 1821. We sold our vessel the *Jupiter*, to agents of Bostwick, a banker from Boston. We got a good price. All the rifles and cannons were taken off the *Jupiter* before the sale. We did not sign our names as we had done in Louisiana and Texas. Pierre took another name, Señor Ricardo de León. He passed himself off as a Mexican coming from the Yucatan. It was not prudent to overtly declare our identity. Spain was still creating difficulties in the midst of the revolution.

We embarked for Guanajay, Cuba, then for the Isle of Pines. We carefully and very secretly examined the important bases of Cuba so as to seize them for ourselves sometime.

We employed three Spaniards imbued with great military and geographic experience. We embarked for Trinidad on September 1821. We captured a Spanish vessel loaded with slaves on its way to Charleston. It was the *Penrith*. We passed ourselves off as Englishmen. The vessel did not drop anchor in Charleston. The slaves were unloaded into little sloops. The sale was made before dawn and before going to Mr. Wade Hampton on October 4, 1821.

I remained in Charleston from that date until November 15. I secretly left for Saint Augustine, Florida, to seek additional supplies. I chose crews and vessels between Florida and Havana to bombard the fort of El Moro Castle in Havana four days before Christmas. The weather was not favorable, misty and rainy, which allowed us to damage the fort, but the Spanish resistance was stronger than I had expected. Three of my vessels arrived nine hours late; they were taken by the Spanish. Havana remained deserted for three days. Most of the inhabitants left the city to hide in the interior of the land. The three vessels that remained with me had to retreat on Christmas day.

The Spanish have never been good in open battles on the sea. The Spanish government has always formed a territorial army because of their many provinces in North and South America. They never trained men for naval combat as the English always have done. Thus, it would have been difficult and a great loss for me to have landed near Havana.

My combat at that city on Christmas Eve had the effect of lessening their reserves but not in a sufficient manner to favor my disembarkation. I beat a retreat and left for the Isle of Pines, where there was no Spanish garrison, only a few customs officers to supervise the sale of slaves. I paid several Spanish soldiers to embark upon my vessels. They were of no value in the battles at sea. They were men of low morals and completely illiterate and superstitious.

In February 1822 I sold two other ships loaded with slaves to an English merchant vessel. They took their cargo to Savannah, Charleston, and Norfolk. I promised the English captain orally not to attack his vessels. I gave my name as Theodore Lucas and a false address in Baltimore.

Pierre and I left for the Isla de Mujeres in March 1822. We captured a rich Spanish vessel; the cargo consisted primarily of maguey fiber, silver ingots and some articles of gold. After a stay of about a month we left for Trujillo, Santo Domingo, then for the islands of Saint Christophe, Nevis, and Guadeloupe. We sold the fibers at Saint Croix, the gold and silver at Guadeloupe. The English are good customers. The Americans were patrolling in the port and watching the coasts. Each week Pierre and I washed our heads with potash and gunpowder, which turned our hair, eyebrows, and mustaches a beautiful red color that made us look like British subjects; we changed our names several times.

We were no longer authorized to be privateers; we no longer seized British vessels. I only desired Spanish ships so as to begin an insurrection in Cuba. In the middle of May 1822, I captured another Spanish vessel near the Cuban coast and gave that vessel to Captain Stinson, who had been in my service for six months. He left for Charleston with the cargo. An American ship approached ours and opened fire. My sailors answered with cannon fire; a confused battle ensued. The cannons fell silent after a half an hour, and I ordered my two vessels to approach the American vessels.

I met with the two American captains and told them that I was at war against Spain, that I was in Spanish waters, and that I had American, English, and Spanish sailors who were working with me in the revolution in Cuba. The American captains accepted my explanations.

Another heavily loaded vessel came from the north. My men seized it. We were never able to tell if it was American or Spanish, for our time was too limited to allow us to burn Galveston, and many Spanish vessels changed their flag for American colors upon entering the Gulf near Florida [sic].

The Spanish and American crews were allied with those of the ships sailing between Cuba and the cities of the Atlantic coast. When those vessels came across our path, we captured them. The captain of one of them was in favor of the Spanish. I challenged him to a duel on board his own vessel. He refused. I slapped him, giving him several blows. I wrote him a note in which I put some instructions to present to the officials of the United States concerning the means and the promise that I was making to seize Cuba and annex it with Florida to the United States. The captain signaled to American vessels that were in the vicinity. Another battle began. I lost 82 men killed. Some were taken prisoner by the Americans.

The American captains thought that I had a base in Charleston, while my bases were the Isla de Mujeres and Cartagena, Grenada, Baltimore, Philadelphia, Camden, New York, and Boston. I had no strong operational base like the one I used to have at Barataria and Galveston. There once was a privateer base at Charleston, but it disappeared like all the others.

I left for Isla de Mujeres in order to make repairs and bring back provisions to the Isle of Pines in June 1822. I made my way around the small islands of Saint Martinique, Saint Christophe, Saint Croix, and Nevis in the months of July and August 1822.

Things were not going well in those months. I captured a Spanish vessel with gold ingots in September 1822. My crews amply pillaged the Spanish vessels. I was on land; a storm arose that destroyed two of my vessels. I boarded one of my vessels that held the cargo of gold, but the storm forced me to disembark. The gold was thrown overboard.

I was taken prisoner by the Spaniards and freed by good friends in the night of December 20, 1822, and kept by my friends until the arrival of an American vessel. I climbed on board. My identity was unknown to the American captain.

I arrived in Charleston in February 1823 and stayed with the Mortimore family for almost a year. My health was not very good. I had a skin irritation and a sore throat. I went to Richmond and Baltimore on business. Pierre stayed in Savannah for a while in the spring of 1823, then he left for the Isla de Mujeres to spend the rest of the year 1823.

I embarked at Charleston for Baltimore in February 1824, then for Saint Augustine in March 1824, then for Vera Cruz in June 1824, and for Cuba in July 1824 to locate the gold thrown overboard during the storm of November 1822. I used fishermen from different places to search the beach. No gold was located; I gave up on it and paid them well. They did not know or recognize me at all. Their leader, John Bustamente, knew me, but he kept them in the dark about my actions. I returned to Vera Cruz in August 1824, then to Isla de Mujeres in September 1824.

I headed toward the Isle of Pines in 1824. I seized a Spanish vessel. My brother Pierre took the 300 slaves to Mobile, Savannah, and Charleston using a borrowed name and flying an English or American flag. The sale was profitable without causing the least notice to Mr. Wade Hampton. After the sale of the slaves, Pierre went to New Orleans in January 1825. He visited his wife and two sons, Cézar and Pierre, then went to the Sabine River from Alexandria. He stayed there until July 1825.

He rejoined me on Isla de Mujeres in August 1825. I set sail for the Isle of Pines and encountered a formation of Spanish warships; a battle followed. I lost many men, and we set sail toward Largo in September 1825.

I decided to liquidate our prizes between the different captains at Guanajay. Another battle took place among the different factions of my men over the distribution of the booty. Several were killed, which caused the rest of the crews to flee. John Betancourt led the faction against my men who remained loyal.

I decided with Pierre to end it all immediately, before the Spanish Army chanced upon our factional war. During the night my brother and I set sail, leaving it to be understood that we had been killed near Guanajay. We headed toward the Isla de Mujeres in November 1825, claiming that I had been stabbed by the leader of the opposing faction.

On New Year's Day of 1826, Sunday, April 9, 1826 [sic], my brother and I decided to give up the cause and split up our property; some for my two sons Antoine and Jean, another portion for my daughter. Pierre shared some portions among his seven children. We relaxed and lived at ease among the Mestizos in Dzilam. Very few among them knew our business, and even when they knew something, they always manifested indifference. No foreign vessel arrived until the month of May; an English vessel arrived and made several inquiries concerning the pirates from Charleston. Those pure-blood Indians and Mestizos avoided giving an answer. The English vessel took on freight at Vera Cruz, and the rumor was spread that the French pirates were on Isla de Mujeres.

We stayed on Isla de Mujeres until April. We loaded our vessels with potash extracted from wood, liquid gum, exotic wood for furniture making, pepper and spices, 126 Zambo slaves, gold plates, and silver ingots for Charleston. We remained in Charleston until September 1826. The property had been split up and given to our children.

My daughter had been married for two years. Her husband Francis Little was a furniture manufacturer. In February 1826 my two sons arrived from France at Saint Croix under borrowed names. The real names of my sons were Jean Antoine, born on January 4,

1801, in Port-au- Prince, and Lucien Adrien, born on May 7, 1802, in Port-au-Prince. My daughter Denise Jeanette was born on August 2, 1804, on board the vessel of my brother. My wife died while giving birth to Denise Jeanette on the vessel near Grande Terre, the same day as the birth. Denise was nursed by a slave woman from Santo Domingo, a domestic servant whom my wife had kept throughout our marriage while Pierre and I were traveling in Europe. My first marriage lasted only a very short time. Most of us were far from home as the world was evolving.

My brother and I stayed prepared for change; we were everywhere without rest; it seemed to us that the entire world was our family, full of wars and revolutions. We were born there, and our homeland had changed from a paradise to a savage island of dark witchcraft. Today it is much worse under complete black mastery. Their ancestors in Africa must, therefore, have been worse. Nothing was done by the officials of Washington, even until now, about the despotic control of the Spaniards on the Cubans or the most degenerate forms of intrigues in Haiti.

My two sons arrived in Charleston in December 1826. They stayed with the Mortimore family near Charleston and the other Mortimore family near Ford Cou, Florida, (Ford Cou is now called Jacksonville.) in April 1827. Lucien and Antoine left Savannah for Philadelphia and stayed with my daughter Denise until December 1827. They went to New Orleans and stayed there until February 1828, then left for the Sabine River and Nagadoches. They went to Baltimore and Philadelphia and stayed there until 1844 and visited in Saint Louis in May 1845. They left for the Antilles in the month of December 1845. My two sons and daughter lived happy and well.

Pierre and I were very busy with a large quantity of merchandise that we had stocked in different ports under borrowed names. We kept four men as secret informers to uncover every conversation and make reports concerning any new event. We conducted our secret missions very well. We only had two vessels operating under private contract with the banking enterprises of Philadelphia.

We decided and pledged never to visit saloons, take the same route twice, never return to Louisiana, Texas, Cuba, or any other Spanish-speaking country. Inquiries were made everywhere concerning our docked vessels and our movements in Baltimore from April 1829 until December 1829. We lived in Richmond from December 1829 until December 1830.

Pierre went to Mobile in December 1830 and stayed there until March 1831. He visited New Orleans in disguise and stayed there a few days with my brother Alexandre, who was happy and satisfied without wanting to accept any merchandise from brother Pierre, who left toward Florida in April 1831, then to Philadelphia in March 1832. He left again for Natchitoches in July 1832 and did not feel well.

My brother was extremely busy in the small villages along the Sabine in Louisiana. He registered a mining claim with the land office in Louisiana and received 11,400 acres in proximity to the Sabine River near the village of Natchitoches. His sons, being adults, were able to receive land grants. There was a mutual agreement among his wife Françoise, his two sons Jean Jacques and Pierre Charles, and two daughters according to which he was to leave his family and live secretly with two other sons, Cézar Edouard and Eugène Louis. He separated from his family in May 1834. His wife Françoise sold many goods in 1834. She died in the month of August 1839 and was buried in the same tomb as her parents in Saint Louis Cemetery in New Orleans.

Jean Laffite

Creve Coeur, Thursday, March 4, 1847

I remained with the Mortimore family close to Charleston from January to July 1831. I moved between July 1831 and December 1831 among Philadelphia, Bridgeton, Boston, and Wilmington, Delaware. At that period I sold enormous quantities of merchandise in those cities and in small cities.

Miss Emma Mortimore and I became engaged for a marriage that was intended to take place in the winter of 1832. I had met her when she was only a child. My daughter opposed our engagement. Emma was very attached to me, even from the time whe she was a little girl. We knew each other well; our marriage took place on June 7, 1832. We agreed never to use our real names so as to hide our identity from the public. A ceremony under disguise proved to be the best.

Emma knows all about my life; a true love of the home has prevailed between us with all our heart and soul. After our marriage we lived in Baltimore for three years. I moved to Cincinnati with my wife and son in May 1835, then to Carandolet in January 1836. Two sons were born: Jules Jean, the elder, in Baltimore on April 4, 1834; Glenn Henri, the younger, was born near this city, Carondolet, on September 18, 1836.

Robert Lucas gave me much information about the West. He was born in Pennsylvania and was my age. He lives in Iowa City. James Lucas of Saint Louis (no relation to Robert Lucas) also helped me very much concerning business practices. James Lucas was more interested in politics and land grants and railroad construction projects.

I granted many loans to start up a business to men who had a gift for leadership. I acquired no property through legal proceedings. I did not wish to have any property transaction on court records. I had a sufficient reserve of gold for my family and my son for a long time. I retired from the cannon powder factory of Olive Street and 29 Levee and Front Street.

My brother Pierre came to Carandolet in May 1834. His two sons Eugène Louis and Cézar Edouard accompanied him; he then left again for Texas and Lafayette Parish, Louisiana. His eldest son Pierre, in a private steamboat business, lived in New Orleans..

My brother Pierre was a grandfather with many grandchildren when he died on March 9, 1844, in the small city of Creve Coeur, Missouri. The burial was in the Wesleyan Cemetery in Saint Louis. He was 64 years, four months, and 19 days old. All of my brothers, Alexandre, Marcus, Henri, and Pierre, are dead. My two sisters María and Anna are dead.

My daughter and her husband live near Saint Louis. They now have five children. My daughter is presently 43. Her hair is all white. Eighteen years ago she was very sick. Her good doctors were William Gibson, 254 Walnut; Doctor William Dewees, 1004 Walnut; Doctor Nathaniel Chapman, 9 House of York in Philadelphia in the year 1830.

My brother and I were very busy in large cities, selling the merchandise that we had stored. Also, we did important business afterward in buying and selling in the years 1832 to 1842.

My wife and daughter are always spinning and weaving; they have become attached to one another since the birth of Jules and Glenn. Wherever my home is located, it is always happy.

I never saw Captain James Campbell again after the day when we burned Galveston. I promised to meet him again at the Isla de Mujeres. He arrived there in April 1821. I gave instructions to the few inhabitants not to reveal the places where my merchandise from our captures was hidden. The captain was a good and loyal Irishman. Captain Campbell left to cruise on his vessel *Hotspur* about a month after my departure from Galveston. He set sail to the island of Trinidad then to the Isle of Pines. He intended to obtain Negroes from the barracks of the Isle of Pines and to find the gold plates and silver bars on the coast of Largo Island. I learned that he was wounded at the Moro Castle Fort of Havana.

Many people sought information from me concerning my brother, and some of them asked me where Captain Campbell, Captain Cochrane, and many others were. I replied to them that everything was worked out between my captains and lieutenants at Galveston, that everything had been done according to their desires, and that an agreement had been made concerning their decisions, of dividing up of ships and articles of value.

I later learned that Captain Cochrane and Captain Campbell had been wounded and taken prisoner near Vera Cruz. Captain Campbell suffered the loss of a great portion of his captures, and his lieutenants Duval and Cox rebelled.

The news from those times is of such a nature that no one can establish the facts. There were also stories that were circulated concerning me. I could not believe my ears. How could I believe the others?

I had no authority or alliance with anyone who left Galveston without me. Questions were asked of me on the subject of the exact spot where I was forced to throw valuables overboard when I was pursued by warships of every government. I could only give the response that I was not trying to recover the valuables thrown overboard because of the moving sands or sandbars and because I had never recorded the exact spot where the plates had been thrown overboard when I was in the midst of a pursuit by vessels because I did not know the exact amount. The men who executed the orders did not know what I had put in the old cannons so as to hide and seal in the gold.

There is a little gold near the island of Largo; near other coasts of Cuba as well, but I cannot tell or direct anyone toward that place to retrieve the gold, for I do not know the exact spot. All that I can say is that some of my officers had some silver hidden on Caillou Island. I do not know the exact spot. The officers never returned.

Seven leagues to the west, two leagues to the north of the Spanish city of Saint Augustine, some of my officers buried a large quantity of gold under my orders. I have no knowledge of the exact spot, for they were taken prisoner and killed by warships, and their papers were destroyed.

Some Spanish silver and some gold remains on Pecan Island. I do not know exactly where. The gold hidden in my warehouses near Catouache was retrieved and moved long ago. Some articles of value remain in Bayou Teche or near New Orleans. I do not know the amount. I am too old to look for the unknown locations of the buried valuables. I now have two men secretly employed to search near New Orleans or Bayou Teche.

After my departure from Galveston for Isla de Mujeres in March 1821, I set sail for Cape Catouache. There I seized two good ships, which cost me a hard fight. Many of my men recruited at Merida were killed. I had it bruited about that I was seriously wounded, then taken to Port Cortes, Honduras, then to Guaiva and Caracas where I was said to have died from wounds in May 1821.

I also had it said that I died in Merida from a bad sickness in 1825. I made some inhabitants believe that I had died in Dzilam in 1826. There were many reasons to create this ruse or invention of subterfuge for those inhabitants of places where intimacy or attachment took too strong a root, especially places where there were mixtures of Indians and Spanish called *Mestizos*, for they attach themselves fervently to whomever they admire or love. In Cuba, those of Spanish origin are not like that; those whom I helped are that way, on the other hand. Since 1825 I lived in greater peace than before, with abundance of means of living and away in a complete personal retirement with my family.

I often think about the good projects that I attempted in the past with all my energy and all my heart in Louisiana and Texas: the legal executions through my courts of Brown, Iuana, and many others who violated my commissions of the privateer marque; Messrs. Clark, Cox, Marotte, and many others who began to mutiny and incite rebellion to destroy my colony. All their desire led to piracy against the good inhabitants of Texas and Louisiana.

My memories of Barataria and Galveston long remained alive in my mind. Presently, the memory has faded but is not forgotten. Texas is now American.

I was told that many people in Louisiana and Texas ask for news of me. I would never want to go to Texas. It would be useless at this late date to find the gold plates and silver ingots thrown overboard at Largo when being pursued by Spanish warships coming from Trinidad. The sands move and change the conditions of the coast. One part was thrown overboard on the coast of Cruz del Padre to the north of Cardenas. It was never possible to locate them afterward. A small part was kept on Pecan Island but never recovered.

I decided never to keep the same men or employ them a second time.

Captain Campbell was a fine man. I often think about him. He was about nine years younger than I. I learned that he left for Boston to spend his last days. He should be about 56 now.

Many people asked me if I was indeed a relative of Mr. Jacques Laffitte of Paris. My only answer was that he was but a distant relation without any dealings with me. I had never seen him when my brothers and I were in France several years in the past. The name Laffitte, Laffite, Lafite, Lafitte comes from the same branch near Switzerland about 500 years ago. Jacques Laffitte died without any property. There are many Laffittes in South Carolina and Georgia; they are French Huguenots. I descend from a French father and a Spanish mother, whose mother was Jewish. My grandmother Zora taught me much universal science. I remember the numerous good friends that I had years ago. Many of them held high positions in the armies of the United States. General Wilkinson was a good confidant; Mr. Wade Hampton and Sam Williams were very close to me in Baltimore, New Orleans, Charleston, and Washington..

Jean Laffite

THE OLD RADICAL

Saint Louis, Monday, April 24, 1848

I left Saint Louis for Europe in June 1847, stopping in various interesting places. I returned to America in January 1848. I was always moving about, dissatisfied, and always wishing for a universal change of man by man.

Personally, I never needed anything. I never had hunger for food products at any time. I was never like many other people who could find contentment in living between four walls without searching out what was beyond the horizon. I could not stand the sight of the multitudes, of the masses, suffering among the better off. I was everywhere when I was only a boy: on land, at sea, in prison; wherever my home might be, it was always happy.

There was even a time when I had my own prisons. I have taken part and been a witness to a cycle of changes of the world. I learned that revolutions were never complete, that Europe was not stabilized, that America was not completed. From the two sides of the Atlantic, problems existed within. I saw that persecution had again returned. I went to Europe; I had meetings with many leaders of the Church, the French Government, and some of the lower classes.

My meetings were brief, in person, but not secret. I stayed with Mr. Louis Bertillon in Paris, sometimes in hotels. I was in Berlin, Brussels, Antwerp, and Amsterdam.

I met Mr. Michel Chevreul, Mr. Louis Braille, Mr. Auguste Thierry, Mr. Antoine de Tocqueville, Karl Marx, Mr. Frederic Engels, Mr. Jules Michelet, Mr. Urbain Le Verrier, Mr. François Guizot, Mr. Louis Daguerre, and many others.

Nothing was peaceful or secure for good legitimate work or for business in Europe. The reasons that encouraged me to spend time and discuss with inventors, historians, and chemists were that I found their conversation and information reasonable.

No one knew the true motivation for my mission to Europe. I even opened a line of escrow credit in the banks of Paris to finance two young men, Mr. Marx and Mr. Engels, for a revolution of the workers of the world. They are at the task and creating laws in Germany, France, Belgium, and Holland. I hope that the new manifest doctrine will overthrow England and Spain, which is now feeble.

It was always my pleasure and intention to take up any cause for liberty, snatched from monarchies or any kingdom. Once I had vessels, and the combined efforts of my opponents outdid and negated my efforts through the fact that my officers accepted gifts, contrary to the rules, discipline, and agreements of the commune of Galveston. I have never regretted the sacrifices and losses they caused me, for there where there is hope or will there is life, and from that day it seems that opportunity and times are better.

England pays enormous amounts of money and uses the intervention of secret agents throughout Europe to avoid colonization. England paid the expenses of the illiterate Irish in order to clear a passage to the United States. One and two months previous, this city received many Irishmen.

Recently, on this Monday, April 24, I spent the greatest part of the day with my grown daughter and her family. I then went to the mixed civilian and military parade, which was followed by good martial music. After the parade we heard the mayor, Mr. Mullanphy, who had taken position on the other side of the street on the east side of the courthouse to speak about the subject of freedom in Europe.

During the evening the crowds assembled on the east side of the tribune to listen to Judge Krum, who spoke on various subjects. I was happy to have been able to bring back from Europe, without anyone knowing, some manuscripts that those two men studied and from which they took notes that helped in the composition of their speeches. They thus learned that Europe has not gotten back on its feet nor recovered economically from the upheavals caused by the Napoleonic Wars and that England kept encouraging the small kingdoms to act like dogs fighting over a bone.

Some people asked me why I was so enthusiastic about the subject of social reforms and of European political economy. First of all, "Every idealist writes about what must happen. Every idealist knows that writings constituted the rudiments of the articulated past." Mr. Marx is an anointed idealist.

I know through personal experience that I found all governments modifying and changing in cycles, either forward or in the opposite direction. England takes the backward path; the United States goes forward.

During the months of January, February, March, and April, the King of Sardinia declares war on Austria. Italy was in rebellion. The Saxons and Hanoverians in Germany had been good to the workers. In Ireland the agitation against the English was considerable, which led to the complete destruction of the partisans of the Charter. The riots in Madrid, Spain, had caused the deaths of many civilians and soldiers. The Emperor of Russia had exiled thousands of people living in Poland.

The greatest portion of the gold that I possess was exchanged and applied to good use and financial assistance of idealists and inventors in France, Germany, Belgium, as well as some American inventors, too. This is my answer to the rare people who know me as to why I have not used the gold in investments for private commercial ventures. My answer is always that the gold I captured and possessed was to be used like an army against those from whom I tore it, the Spaniards and English and the entire world that adores the yellow metal. What is the reality, the least-known danger of all humanity, when it is amassed and adored to the point of creating greed?

Moses warned his people against the curse that was going to

befall them. Warnings and good teachings have been made and transmitted to the present from times immemorial. Every nation and every savage tribe has had, and still has, good guidance at the core of its higher ethics and codes, but *no one* has ever discovered or written down the true causes nor the evils of men among men: "Exploitation of man by man." I formed an escrow association in Paris to come to the aid of the two young men, Mr. Marx and Mr. Engels, who would discover, write down, and record the causes of human progress as well as the effects of the hostilities and failures of the past.

People wondered why I felt an interest in the masses of future generations. The answer: Most of the gold that I possess was dug up and ripped from the earth upon the hardened backs of Mestizo Indians reduced to slavery in Peru in South America and in Mexico during the time when those provinces were under the iron fist of the Spaniards.

My answers: No man can live two days in a row in the same way, for different influences and desires possess and dominate within him. I only understand the great laws of nature by its effects, which I conceive through vegetation planted in the ground that receives appropriate light, heat, and humidity to make it grow and produce its products.

I feel happy; no one has found out what I personally possess. I have given presents to help other people, and now I feel more enthusiastic. My thoughts are always busy on the subject of future generations so that they will have "life, liberty, and the pursuit of happiness" and love, peace, and tranquility to reign in complete mastery to infinity.

Jean Laffite

Saint Louis, Thursday, February 22, 1849

Many people asked me why I used to sell slaves so cheaply and then changed my mind on the question of slavery at a later date. My answer: The slaves whom I captured on the English and Spanish vessels were already civilized slaves. Most of them were born with English or Spanish blood in their veins.

My privateer captains captured English and Spanish vessels loaded with slaves and merchandise that was being transported from one port to another and intended for speculation by the English and Spaniards who intended to sell them along the ports of the Atlantic coast.

"I strongly hated England and Spain."

I equally hated the changing and speculative laws concerning taxes upon revenues that fall heavily upon affluence, taxes that were set upon the mass of people ready for progress. Such were the reasons that were paramount to me and caused me to snatch away the slaves from brutal speculators and release them later with other merchandise at reduced prices to those with the greatest need.

I was opposed to the fiscal laws——created by one or two men—— to impose upon the people, without a referendum and vote, without the least right to speak out, to protect the legal sales of Negro slaves by traffickers who were exercising a monopoly along the states of the Atlantic coast and, at the same time, forbidding sales of slaves in Louisiana

Through my experience I kept them from the most savage speculators on the high seas. I sold them for almost nothing in Louisiana and Texas to owners of great plantations. Mr. Guy Champlain bought 100 and 200 at a time. Mr. Wade Hampton would buy 300 and 500 at a time. The Bowie brothers bought a certain number of them each time. They re-sold the Negroes at a profit, which I was very far from approving. The Negroes that I had captured had already been slaves under the exploitation of the Spanish and English. I have never visited any African province or continental territory. I had never seen any Negroes coming directly from Africa. All the Negroes who were captured and brought to my commune were in the majority accustomed to speaking bad French and a mixture of Spanish. Some spoke bad English; they had been captives on English vessels. The majority of the slaves belonging to me received money according to their color, their

morals, and their upbringing. Absolute slavery cannot long endure.

Jean Laffite

Belleville, Monday, September 24, 1849

My wife Emma was a member of the antislavery party of Philadelphia. I made some monetary contributions to that party. Reasons: I do not approve of absolute slavery, feudal servitude, or wage
slavery. I approved of liberty according to the knowledge, needs,
and abilities of men.

All the men of the jungle or mountain forests ought to undergo methods of rigorous training for some kind of work. But!
Despite that, it is slavery. Such is the name that anyone can give it.
I approve of it, but I do not like it, nor can I approve the subjuga-
tion of any race or sect if they respect the full measure of progress.
No man or system of government can hold men under its control
or in slavery when the slaves adapt to a universal education and
science. No man can raise a Negro to the full limit of his abilities
and then succeed in imposing his will on him. I know and can
affirm that I am the only, unique man who has had more contact
with and managing of Negroes than any other man.

Governments ought to grant a territorial compensation where
slavery exists. The Negro can and wants to contribute to his own
progress under the good direction of governments around him.
But the Negro cannot make any progress without written records
or laws of obligation having taken form under the framework of a
good constitution.

No race of humans can progress without annals of its heritage
that it can follow. Not all men invent. Inventors are idealists, and
very few of them are to be found. They are persecuted when they
are discovered and known, whether they are inventors of good laws
for progress or of tools for progress.

Jn Laffite

Chester, South Carolina,
Tuesday, March 19, 1850

Stories have been circulated in Louisiana, and they have been brought back to me by friends worthy of trust, that I am said to have silver and gold hidden in the sandy shores of all the islands along the Gulf coast. If I or anyone else really wanted to advise and persuade that there were not any valuables hidden among the islands of the Gulf, there would be more investigations and more people searching and digging in the hunt for valuables.

It is true. There are some caches in places, but I do not have the least idea of the exact locations and would not wish to waste my time by trying to discover the lost valuables or buried treasure. I indeed have many valuable articles near New Orleans, buried in some little estuary, tucked away, and unknown by everybody but me.

I know people only too well! Many people are very common and with an inferior mentality when excited by others. Horses are difficult to pull from a fire; furry animals like the racoon and fox are attracted by the shiny, brilliant surfaces of traps. A noisy parrot repeats what it hears said. A monkey imitates the actions of men. A proud lion is charmed by white colors and piercing music. Songbirds are subjugated by snakes. Many people are led on bad, false paths without reward or full guarantee . . .

In no way am I in a condition to inform or advise whomever it may be at this late hour about hidden valuables or treasures. Would I do it? I would be crucified or tied to a tree and burned alive by all the mad men who think alike today and deeply regret and weep the next. Wisdom arrives with age.

History repeats itself for good and evil. There is always a beginning of birth and ripening death for all things. Chattel slavery is now ready to be abolished. Wage slavery will mature because of more and more numerous inventions and will be abolished in various ways in four generations. Wage slavery cannot exist under the same form or any form. If wage slavery is subjected to any, or the same old pattern, that would bring about rebellion in the entire world.

Inventions develop and endure. An international education will be necessary to face up to and march side by side with progress and the inventions which occur. The dust that everyone walks on will be worked and transformed into base metal. Machines will be invented to write words more quickly on paper than could be written by 20 human hands with a quill.

Three years ago I made contact with some doctors, chemists, inventors, men dedicated to astronomical research in Europe. I am fond of talking about progress and development. All great men desire changes and total progress for the good and well-being of generations to come. I am one of those men who desire to see the cycle of change—whether I be alive or dead. When I am dead, my spirit will rise up far away and right afterwards to be a witness to the changes. When I continue to live, I will only be able to measure the changes with time.

The ignorant do not understand or know anything about time and space. The ignorant only know time as a factor of work, rest, and sleep. The ignorant only know "time and space" according to sunrise in the east and sunset in the west. Time is a measure of human consciousness. Space is the measure of human prolongation by time. Without the knowledge of time and space, great men would not be able to exist with progressive ideals.

All the animals of the lowest species, all the life of the fish in the rivers and oceans have no measure of consciousness in "time and space." Human beings who live in a primitive state in different parts of the world measure time by the sun in full day and seasons and temperature by the moon. They measure space by rivers and distant mountains, but not by numerical calculation.

I never have believed personally in the principles of perpetual slavery. I have never approved of the idea of the slave trade and keeping of slaves with the goal of making a profit or speculating according to their well-being. I would like to see the slaves develop their talents with the goal of procuring for themselves the purchase of their freedom. There is nothing impossible. Without traditional talents and historical annals, humanity, that is to say all living beings, would return to the time of the club and cave or again to the era of the Dark Ages.

Good words of truth, figures, and facts presented to men endowed with good sense and healthy intelligence could lead human beings in a march forward toward progress that would cause them to invent more and more; to learn how to live and suppress their ignorance of existence in order to lighten their burden so as to live powerfully, better, and more easily; to liberate them from the yoke of others; and to eliminate all illnesses. From there, man can and wants to live his existence without suffering, lamentations, or pleas for pity.

Kindness is the language the deaf can hear and mutes can understand. No man today can yet explain the process of transformation beyond his understanding, of tropical birds shining with all kinds of color, nor the birds of far northern regions covered with dark gray or black. Man only knows the effects of nature. He has drawn upon and penetrated many causes and effects of nature. However, many causes still remain mysterious and to be unraveled.

A man can hear the pulsating rhythm of the wheels under a wagon, yet he will not know what is in the wagon as long as he will not go look at it. The same principles are applicable to the written annals of truth: facts and figures. No man knows what exists in good books on the pages between their rough covers until he goes on his own to see and read them.

Poverty is a precursor to crime. Ignorance is the precursor to all evil. To suppress the exploitation of man by man, I have always maintained the idea that the so-called criminals, those created by poverty, could become good citizens. Poverty is the first cause of all crimes. Let poverty disappear and crimes will cease to exist.

Half of the world is ignorant about the other half. There are many people who have neither taste nor interest in the future of public affairs, no more than some people have either natural inclination or the ear for music. There are many people who cannot take into consideration the feelings of others any more than many people who can tell one color from another. There are many unjust people without principle, who cannot tell good from evil. Music can be heard; colors can be seen.

Feelings can be considered through appropriate community social compacts. Justice can be rendered similarly for everyone with whom it is concerned through the will and agreements of communities, above all through an appropriate education.

Thirdly, by means of an appropriate education in such a way that everything can and must have an aesthetic value, as well as a good differentiation among all things. Good schools for everyone up to the age of 16 will engender good learning, and evils will cease. At that time, every man and woman should carry a registration number.

Every man holding a position of public trust should have to post a bond. The law should also forbid him from accepting presents or any fraudulent undertaking. He should also be forbidden to take part in secret meetings behind closed doors.

I have always been aware of the difference of social classes, and I have always adhered to the principles of liberty that assure to each and every one the total possession of the fruits of their labor and the pursuits of their desires. I have never had any bitterness toward the poor, any more than a sieve can hold water. I have always avoided politicians whose company could only have been boredom and monotony, for nothing can equal the resentment of politicians whom one disdains at the height of their power.

Many people have asked me how many duels I had fought and how I could manage to come out the winner of each duel. I fought 17 duels. The second was the hardest and the most difficult with a free Spanish quadroon on his ship *Aires de Mora*. The other duels were easy.

My only answer concerning the subject of skill with sword fighting was: First, look straight at the eyes of the opponent and not his sword point. Every ingenious and well-meaning man can always succeed in whatever he tries; always look straight in the eyes and not at the hands because they can always fool the eyes.

Second, try to understand a man by his way of looking, his eyes being an indication of his inner being. No man can see his own measure. He who is devoid of intelligence cannot see it. Let's take the case of someone who is color blind. The colors are visible, but he cannot recognize them. The completely blind can deny the existence of light because he does not see it. All my adversaries in duels revealed some inferiority and reminded me of the distracted, the color blind, and the totally sightless.

I never provoked or forced anyone to a duel or to the slightest irritation. When I was provoked, I would challenge to a duel.

Jn Laffite

Saint Louis, Tuesday, June 4, 1850

Many people ask about my features, characteristics, gifts; all that I can say is that I have been endowed with patience, concentration for command, resoluteness to surmount weakness coupled with endurance. I was always bold, ready to seize opportunities, and strongly desirous to see things move along rapidly.

All that remained immobile, stationary, or caused failure got on my nerves. I am very gifted for devoting myself to the subject of peace and harmony and in favor of maintaining friendships through virtue of my innate traits, independently of thought. I have never had any empathy for the brutal.

I am not superstitious. No one knows who I was, but as for myself, I knew it well. In truth, I was safer when I had dealings with a good-for-nothing than with certain persons who in other circumstances became reprobates.

I am always being asked why I stopped helping politicians. One very simple, sufficient reason is that I am an idealist and not a politician, a member of a degenerate parliamentary faction, and that I have no desire to hang on to old two-faced principles. I have always acted rightly, knowing well that the majority of those with

whom I had business were the worst liars and disguised hypocrites, whose envious and greedy minds only dreamed about getting the most lucrative public offices.

I have always said that the common law ought to force the
clergy to register in order to keep the Church from spreading superstitions and baseless fears concerning the depths of the earth
and the immensity that extends around our planet, as well as prevent hypocrites from profiting while upsetting the public. When
hypocrisy manages to create fears and superstitions, freedom flees.

I do not know what the reports concerning me at this late date
prove. I do not know either what happened to the seven English
letters that I had set aside with joy to help the verifications of the
secrets of the British invasion. I do not know if Mr. Blanque, Mr.
Claiborne, Judge Hall have caused these letters to disappear. They
have probably been destroyed and have disappeared from the files
at the present time.

Many people from Louisiana showed themselves grateful to
me. Those who were in power were hostile to me and very critical.
They were favored by the savior of a nation, then later by the peace
treaties of compromise and those private patents of exploitation
and commerce which will soon cause the birth of conflicts that
will tear apart the nation.

I no longer know much concerning the regions of Texas and
Louisiana. Texas is now an American state. I brought assistance
with much good will to many people in Texas, Louisiana, Cuba,
and many other corners of the world. My treasures that I had to
burn will be avenged by the fifth generation of those aggressive
birds of prey who chased me away.

The pen is stronger than any weapon, and I am going to give
all my resources to the men of Germany and France to form a
workers' manifesto for liberty.

Man does not control the length of his life by good thoughts,
but by his appetite. Half of what he eats keeps him alive; the other
half kills him. Pure air and liquids are the first food of the newborn
and the last ones of the dying. Government officials can control

and discipline a population with good food, a good guarantee of recompense, instead of words or a utopia found in a dictionary.

All philosophers and artists want to be reformers, many losing their head. No one knows my past. Sometimes I am taken to be an Englishman, sometimes a Spaniard or Frenchman, on the occasion of Saint Patrick's Day, an Irishman.

We always know what to do after things are done. It took me so long to become strong and assure my personal development that I never took the time to criticize those who work honestly for their earnings but only in order to give them the attitude that they were as satisfied with themselves as I was with myself.

The years have not yet taken hold of me due to the fact that I have never given up my ideals based on the predilection for liberty. I have never had worries or fears. I have never, because of doubt and despair, lowered my head while asking time to reverse itself. I have never compromised myself nor sold my soul to the devil.

I possess a good temperament, vigorous emotions, a courage stronger than my timidity, and the implacable determination to restrain the infantile appetites of the members of the royal families of Europe, who only wish to determine from those appetites the desire of the popular masses to become a sovereign state with a universal, cultivated government [sic].

You can always form an opinion of a stranger by your generosity. If he abuses your generosity, then he is not worth the effort of giving him your trust and good will when he is with you or in your entourage. When strangers arrived at my table, I always introduced myself by saying: "Permit me right off and in all hospitality to sit down with you so that I can reserve that portion of myself between my mustache and my mouth for the pleasures of the mouth without any other duty farther away than my elbow, and I assure you that you will be mindful of my company and my well-being."

Clothing: a coat of neutral color with a bit of *peau de soie* in the material, a well rounded collar, a stylish necktie, and polished boots.

The head high, well supported on a good-sized neck on wide shoulders, such was my appearance and bearing which caused difficulty in guessing my nationality. The English and Spaniards could never do the same.

I have had long struggles and am happy to be finally near my goal. "I love liberty." I no longer regret anything of the past, for my generosity expended among some who cried out and became implacable against me.

I often wonder at this moment how many people in this very city of Saint Louis, even those so-called educated ones residing on the hill above the river, know the Great Manuscript as the precursor of the body of the nation.

Saint Louis is a very beautiful city, set on a pretty site. Its politics are corrupt; the fault lies, as it does everywhere, with its development and rapid growth.

The railroad is a great invention and a good reason to suppress slavery and effect new changes. Today there is a new railroad from the city to the Meramac River; it will be lengthened in the future. Mr. Chouteau wants to sell me his share. Mr. Lucas is very worried about his share. I have offered the present of a large quantity of gunpowder to blow up boulders. Mr. Ward, Mr. Kingsley, and Mr. Peabody seem to me to very honest, nice men to take care of the railroad. I refused to buy the share of another person. I have indeed granted some mutual loans. I shall never see the money again, but I do not regret it.

In this city I have many good friends. Mr. Benoist, Mr. Soulard, Mr. Kilburne on the sidewalk opposite to the big courthouse, and many other good friends. They know my true past; many others are unaware of it.

Good families in this city own Negro slaves whom my vessels had brought as spoils from Spanish vessels. Very few know anything about me. Mr. M. Js. Morrison of this city had bought slaves and wrought iron for decoration. Mr. François Saucier bought slaves for his property; he also bought salt. Mr. Belamus Hayden and Mr. Antoine La Forge bought some slaves in Madrid, Missouri.

Mr. Hunter (William) was a buyer of slaves. He lived near Madrid, Missouri. Mr. Beebe bought some slaves from my agent, Mr. D. Martin 38 years ago (in Donaldsonville, Louisiana). Mr. John Darby owns two of those slaves, whom I met recently. They are now about 65 years old.

Their Spanish masters cut off the index finger of each hand before they were captured by privateers. I talked with those two slaves three years ago. They remember their capture and sale at Barataria. Negro slaves captured from English or Spanish vessels a few years ago by my captains still carry certain identification marks on their bodies: either scars or toes or fingers or a part of an ear cut off.

It is a very deeply rooted instinct in man to mark his personal property of value, not for the simple need of identification but for the pleasure of satisfying their desire to see decoration. A man or a woman with earrings is an example of display. Certain men have the instinct of marking, cutting, or engraving everywhere they go with the goal of satisfying their curiosity so that others may follow the straight or evil path. The Spaniards were the most clever with this method when they explored and exploited all of Mexico and South America.

The civilized Aztec Indians of Mexico and the Inca Indians of Peru were hardly superior to their own populace before the arrival of the Spaniards to conquer them.

Sailors at sea have marked young turtles to satisfy the curiosity of others at a later date; men have marked birds to please others at a later date. Giving and leaving behind markings and written annals for progress so as to lighten burdens for the good and the best is a great divine blessing to others and to generations to come. It is bad, and beneficial for no one, to write on, brand, cut, engrave on, or disfigure any animal, path, or trail for others and for generations to come to overthrow time, science, and progress in order to add more influence for the bad and the worst.

I have met many Negro slaves in small towns close to this city who carry the same marks as at that time of their capture by my captains 40 years ago and sold at reduced prices to buyers from New Orleans up to this city. I chatted with some old slaves who were property of the Vancourt brothers, living in their hotel on Morgan Street. Mr. Chambers has a hall for the buying and selling of Negroes near the post office on Chestnut Street. Mr. Gordon took some old Negroes there to exchange and I identified them as coming from Barataria some 38 years ago.

I had a conversation with Isaac Moses about three years before his death. He convinced me in 1815 not to try to get back some of my property. He explained to me that he had never been reimbursed for his financial help from the time of the revolution against the English. He also explained that S.H. Solomon had never been reimbursed for the economic assistance he brought to General Washington. That conversation in 1815 weakened my resolve in Washington City at that time. I owe many things to Mr. Dupont de Nemours of Wilmington for the good services that they rendered me many years ago in December 1815 from Washington City.

Now everybody is on the road for the new gold fields of California. All the wagons are heading for the West. It seems that everyone is going to leave the city. Everyone is going crazy for gold; many people have left the city toward California for the gold rush, and others will follow.

Certain among them will never return. Mr. Clemens is doing great business selling canvas for tents and for wagons to all those who come to town and go to California.

Abel Lenar and François Le Sieur had slaves for a long time; they still have the same ones. I retired from the cannon powder factory on Front Street. The Laflin brothers are running it; I help them with loans.

I have only one son, Jules. I will have enough for him and his family when he grows up. My other two sons have enough for themselves. For several years my son Antoine was a school teacher, interpreter on Prunes Street in Philadelphia. No one in Philadelphia knew he was my son.

In my correspondence with George Graham, I told him that my son Antoine was coming to help me. My grandchildren have enough to start out for themselves. My brothers-in-law are still helped by me if they need assistance. The brothers of my wife are successful in business in the areas of pharmacy and steamboats.

A new fort named Livingston has been built on land of Grande Terre that was once my property. My brother Alexandre and Uncle Reyné helped Captain Decatur somewhat when our commune was at Grande Terre. A part of the powder was bought from Pierre Dupont De Nemours five leagues downstream from Philadelphia; I gave some cannons to Captain Decatur.

I am nearly 68 now. I like to cut wood. Each morning I cut wood for 30 minutes.

About a year ago my family and I returned from an enjoyable trip to the area of Washington, Missouri, and Saint Charles.

About five years ago my wife and I , with our two children, took a ride along Front Street in Saint Louis, a carriage ride on the hill and around the lake; we contemplated many interesting panoramas. There was a complete contrast between the top of the hill and low Front Street, where workers rubbed elbows with slaves. All the shops had saloons; men drank whiskey, bargain price poison, while swearing and eating pigs' snouts and feet. Garlic, tobacco, and unending dry sausages were mixed with the liquors and poison whiskey. Workers devoid of feelings and morals fought or shoved each other against the brick walls or lay in the dankness of the filthy streets.

Such things did not occur in my commune many years ago. I kept my men disciplined with a better morality. The odor of rotten meat, cheap liquor, and curses kept many people at a distance in Saint Louis. I can only blame the city bureaucrats. My son-in-law, Francis Little, explains the entire situation the way I found it.

My family and I went to the home of Harriet Greene for dinner on Main Street near Chestnut Street. We followed the north side of Front Street up to Morgan Street, turned to the south toward Main Street up to the building of the new office of the Pacific

Railroad. We drove our team to the house of Mr. Daniel Davis on Fourth Street on the corner of Franklin Street to have dinner.

My son Jules and my two grandsons, Eugene and Francis, have learned German. Mr. Jacob Philipson was their teacher. Mr. Bonfils was also one of the teachers of my son Jules. Mr. Edouard Case is trying to teach music to my son Jules; my grandson Francis also learns music with Mr. Chase. My son Jules and Jacques Clemens ride horses and ride about on theirs around the Fourteenth Street Park. Jules and William Morrison go to the woods to hunt wild animals.

My wife and I had a meeting with Mr. Jules Hatawa to have a faithful portrait of our family executed. She claims that a new invention exists allowing the making of "Daguerre" photographs with a small box, which are reproduced on sheets of thin black metal.

I receive many long letters from a young man, Mr. Vieuxtemps; he is a musician living in Belgium.

No one should either buy or possess more than is necessary to satisfy his needs and desires, but should buy only the essential.

Dr. Forbes pulled out a few of my teeth four years ago in his small room on Second Street. His office burned 13 months ago. I remain with 20 good teeth. My wife had Dr. Brown pull two of her teeth on Chestnut Street two weeks before the fire.

My family and I were staying at the old Prairie house situated near Olive Road four miles west of Saint Louis, as well as the Shackett house located about 55 rods to the west of the Prairie house.

Mr. Freeman Little, the undertaker is a member of my son-in-law's family.

My son Jules paid Elmer 25 dollars to steal the slave Stephan after the death of his owner, Mrs. Smith.

I loved humans, and they loved me. I was young, and I knew that the power I had could not last forever. I tried to create the communes while I had the chance. We had as our goal the weakening of the Spanish armies by taking their seagoing vessels from them. Florida was abandoned because of its weakness, thanks to the action of my privateer fleet against the Spanish ships on the ocean.

Two hundred fourteen years after the date of my birth, the foundations will be shaken and afterward burned by the human being and his mosaic laws of exploitation. Europe will experience seven republics, and the eighth will coordinate the East from Eurasia. In the last days the smallest republic will win the universe.

Jn Laffite

Clayton, Thursday, October 17, 1850

The burning of the city 17 months ago caused an immense illumination. The stone factory building on Front Street did not burn. There was a big discount sale on canvas after the fire. My son Jules and my grandson Edouard stayed up very late at night to watch the fire. They found eight little Negro slaves, children. They took the eight slave children with them (their ages ranging from seven to ten) to the other side of the river to the home of a Negro and his wife. He took them to Edwardsville. They found a place there to work for wages as free Negroes.

There are women who can sin for love and, through pity, cause death to many. There are men who can love many women, but will risk their hides for one who will spurn them.

The fire began at nine forty-five in the evening of May 17, 1849, on the steamboat, the *White Cloud*, anchored at Cherry Street. The fire was caused by a man named Charles Blount, who had given cheap liquor to two Negro slaves to cause them to quarrel over some carrots of tobacco to steal and smoke; that was the cause of a small open box of gunpowder catching fire and bursting into flames in the fight between the two Negro slaves. The flames spread from the *White Cloud* southwest to the steamboat *Ed Bates* and from there to 21 other steamboats; and 13 small boats that had anchored in the basin, after being cut free, went down the river and caused the flames to spread to buildings, which caused 430 houses and buildings to be completely burned down to the inside of their brick walls.

No one knows exactly how many people lost their lives; many slaves were cast out to the shore and covertly crossed the river to the free states by using wood that they clung to and made their way to the other side.

One of my secret agents caught up with Charles Blount in Cape Girardeau, Missouri, while he was trying to escape and disappear on a steamboat for Memphis. That was the end of Charles Blount, who was really the cause of the fire and who no one ever knew was the guilty party. It would never have done any good or been of much value to reveal his name, for he was doubtless a man secretly in the employ of an insurance agent in competition and politicians arguing like merchants for offices of public trust, who abused the illiterate, powerless public.

For those reasons it would have done no good to reveal him to those from whom he received secret pay, for it would have become a long lasting scandal in the courts to expose those in the bureaus of the city who would then probably never again receive help to rebuild the city.

The remainder of the city was in such great confusion and hysteria after the fire that no one would believe or could be believed by anyone else if the particulars of the causes were revealed, as there were many insurance companies who were at knife point in their competition and who were linked to the corrupt politicians in the public offices downtown.

The steamboat *S.B. Autocrat* was visited and inspected for illnesses upon its arrival in Saint Louis on May 17, 1849. It was not prudent to live in the city, for the city water was unhealthful to drink and had been the cause of an epidemic that had taken away more than 4,000 lives.

My son Lucien was a student for a time while he was at the University of Saint Louis when it became a school at Second and Market in the E. Alvarez Building. He studied history and languages.

I lent money to the highest bidder at the sale of the property of Mr. Joseph Dawson, put up for sheriff's sale in front of the Court House on December 4, 1846.

Six years ago the British government established opium houses in Hong Kong, which were to be open from 16 to 18 hours a day and which is one of the worst misfortunes of permitting, under a written law, the opportunity of exploitation of weak pagans by an increasing number of pious hypocrites.

I met some trusted friends who were arriving on the steamboat *Domain* on November 10, 1845.

I always registered in hotels under the false name of William Whiteridge when I traveled from one city to another. A fire broke out in Matanzas, Cuba. My American hotel, a large cafe, and 49 houses were entirely destroyed. On June 8, 1849, I gave William Shelton and C. White the sum of 500 dollars as aid to fire victims.

Illiterate men are like wheelbarrows, and not very good, unless they are pushed. Some people are like small boats floating downstream and are not very good unless they are forced to row upstream. Some are like bubbles in the air. No one can say where they are going to break. Some are like bags filled with air and ready to burst. An intelligent man is like a good watch face covered with real gold and very inventive while doing good work

The Englishman who got in touch with me for meetings and offers never learned that my brother Pierre was in prison during the summer months of 1814, as was presumed and bruited about in New Orleans.

Numerous marriages were celebrated in my communes in the form of a simple registration outside the law, without the benefit of priests or pastors and the benefit of religious sanction. All the marriages that were so celebrated continue in much better harmony than those that were celebrated under the auspices of sacred rites, be they pious or pagan.

I paid for 200 barrels of sulfur which arrived on the steamboat *Helen*, on July 23, 1845, and also for 420 barrels which arrived on the *Palestine* on April 20, 1846.

I have described my past: the missions that I accomplished, my true convictions. The greatest part of my wealth has been sacrificed without regret so that others may do good work , all of it without a trace, without leaving my name.

I do not hesitate from the beginning to be positive in my writings and my journal. I fervently believe that all future events can be guided with precision and certainty.

If God wishes to love the fifth generation to come, he will unveil the intentions and the spirit of the dead. And with my entire help!

Down with the British Dragon.
Monday, December 2, 1850
Jn Laffite

ENDNOTES

1   The spelling of the surname Laffite is a controversy in itself. According to the *Handbook of Texas*, it was spelled Laffite with an acceptable variant spelling of Lafitte. There are many documented variations and even common misspellings. The Laffite Society of Galveston chose the spelling of Laffite since that was how Jean Laffite normally signed his name.

2   Alice D. Le Plongeon, *Here and There in Yucatan* (New York: Book Composition & Electrotyping Co., 1886), 7.

3   Charles Adams Gulick, Jr. and Winnie Allen, eds., *The Papers of Mirabeau Buonaparte Lamar* (Austin: Von Boekmann-Jones Co. For Texas State Library, 1925), 4, pt. 2: 22.

4   "Reminiscences of Early Texans", *Southwestern Historical Quarterly* 4, no. 3 (January 1903): 252. This article is from "Recollection of Early Texans" collected by J. H. Kuykendall in 1857 which were included in the Austin Papers.

5   Ibid

6   W. Eugene Hollon and Ruth Laphan Butiler, eds. *William Bollaert's Texas* (Norman: University of Oklahoma Press, 1956), 16-17.

7   Ibid. 160. William Bollaert also wrote "Life of Jean Laffitte, the Pirate of the Mexican Gulf", *Littell's Living Age* 32 (March 1852): 433-446.

8   H. Yoakum, *History of Texas* (New York: Redfield, 1855, reprint, Austin: Steck Co.,1935), 1: 204. Yoakum's sources were *DeBows Review* (October 1851), "Jim Campbell", *United Service Magazine* (1852) and a letter from Thomas M. Duke to F. Pinchard, May 1843.

9   John Henry Brown, *History of Texas, 1685-1892* (St. Louis: L. E. Daniell Publisher, 1893), I: 71.

10 Joseph L. Clark, *A History of Texas, Land of Promise* (Dallas: D.C. Heath and Company, 1939), 77. Clark used the spelling Lafitte.

11 Newspaper articles including photographs have been published of the grave marker for Jean Laffite where the author claimed to have been shown the final resting place. None of these have been verified and are dismissed by serious researchers. The earliest newspaper account entitled "Lafitte and His Associates" was from the *Galveston Civilian & City Gazette* in 1855. It stated "Lafitte afterwards, located on the coast of Yucatan, at the island of

Mugeres, where he died, according to traveler Stevens, leaving a widow and a hecatomb of turtle shells to honor his memory." Source, *The Papers of Mirabeau Buonaparte Lamar*, 4, pt. 2: 30. Some researchers contend that the Laffites and their associates purposely planted stories of their death so that all could escape prosecution from the authorities and retire to obscurity.

12   Michel Antochiw, Merida, Yucatan, to Dorothy McD Karilanovic, Galveston, August 22, 1995, Letter in Spanish and English translation, Laffite Society Research Collection, Sam Houston Regional Library and Research Center, Liberty. This collection hereafter cited as LSRC,SHRLRC.

13   Ibid.; and "Year of 1821 Summary Investigation Against the Englishman "Don" Jorge Schumph Relative to the Pirate "Don" Pedro Lafitte, His Death and His Burial in the Port of Dzilam", *Centro de Apoyo a la Investigacion Historica de Yucatan, Documentos Peninsulares* (Merida, Yucatan, Mexico: Instituto de Cultura de Yucatan, January 1995), LSRC,SHRLRC.

14   Antochiw to Karilanovic, August 22, 1995, LSRC,SHRLRC.

15   Bethany Enald Bultman, *New Orleans* (Oakland, CA: Compass American Guides, 1994), 42.

16   When or if he changed his name from Lafflin to Lafitte is unknown and genealogical research so far has been unproductive. This is an area that needs further research and unless evidence exists, John A. Lafitte never used the surname of Lafflin.

17   Mrs. Ray Thompson to Pamela Grunewald, October 15, 1975, letter; and Mrs. Ray Thompson, Gulfport, MS, to Pamela Grunewald, Miami, OK, December 12, 1975, LSRC,SHRLRC. Mrs. Ray Thompson is Sue Thompson. Pamela Grunewald is Mrs. Lee Grunewald and Pamela Keyes. Sue Thompson stated both years in different letters.

18   Mrs. Ray Thompson to Pamela Grunewald, December 12, 1975, LSRC,SHRLRC.

19   Ibid.

20   John Andrechyne Lafitte, Certification of Birth Facts, May 13, 1947, Jean Laffite Collection, Sam Houston Regional Library and Research Center, Liberty. Collection hereafter cited as JLC,SHRLRC. Note: This author has not searched the local government records of Kansas or Nebraska for documentation of John Andrechyne or Leon Jean Lafitte. However, several other scholars and genealogists have done so without finding census or other records. Thus, one avenue of research has so far proved to be unfruitful. The majority of states did not require the recording of birth and death certificates until after 1900 and even the early laws were not enforced of followed systematically until the 1920s.

21 St. Louis City Hall to John A. Lfitte, Kansas City, March 6, 1948, letter, LSRC, SHRLRC. Note: This is the only time that John A. Lafitte used the name Lafflin in a letter and he is referring to the fact that only Jean Laffite used it as an alias. John A. never stated that he, his father or grandfather used the surname Lafflin. Many people refer to John A. Lafflin when there is apparently no proof for it.

22 John Lafitte, Kansas City, to Charles van Ravenswey [sic], St. Louis, June 19, 1948, letter, LSRC,SHRLRC. Note: This is the only time that John A. Lafitte used the name Lafflin in a letter and he is referring to the fact that only Jean Laffite used it as an alias. John A. never stated that he , his father or grandfather used the surname Lafflin. Many people refer to John A. Lafflin when there is apparently no proof of it.

23 Clyde H. Porter, Kansas City, to Charles van Ravenswaay, St. Louis, November 21, 1951, letter, LSRC, SHRLRC. Note: Frank Glenn told this story to Clyde H. Porter who passed it on to Ravenswaay, not a rare occurrence in this saga.

24 Charles van Ravenswaay, St. Louis, to Mr. Lewis, Alton, IL, November 18, 1953, LSRC,SHRLRC.

25 Stanley Clisby Arthur, *Jean Laffite, Gentleman Rover* (New Orleans, Harmanson, 1952); Madeleine Fabiola Kent, *The Corsair, A Biographical Novel of Jean Lafitte, Hero of the Battle of New Orleans*, (Garden City, New York: Doubleday & Company, Inc., 1955). Note: Madeleine Kent was the pen name for Mrs. Espinosa. At this time this author has not documented that in fact this is the same Espinosa as the wife of the Cuban Kansas City representative, but it appears that Madeleine Kent is the same person that is referred to in Frank Glenn's story. It is unknown how much of the "trunk archives" was shared with either author. See, Memorandum of Agreement, September 3, 1952, between Doubleday & Company, Inc., Madeleine Kent de Espinosa, William Espinosa, John A. Lafitte [sic], JLC, SHRLRC.

26 Lewis E. Harris, Director Harris Laboratories, Lincoln, NE, to Mrs. Luola Surratt, Kansas City, June 2 1955, letter, Jean Laffite Collection File, Sam Houston Regional Library and Research Center, Liberty. Hereafter cited as JLCF,SHRLRC. Note: John A. Confused things by having the return letter addressed to one of his in-laws, his wife being Lacie Surratt Lafitte.

27 David C. Mearne, Washington D.C., to John A. Laffite, Kansas City, September 5, 1956, JLCF,SHRLRC. Note: "Dear Mr. _____ " is how this letter begins. Again, another mystery is why John A. obliterated his name on this letter, but the envelope is addressed John _____ (again whited out) Kansas City. It is unclear which book was examined. Some researchers have attempted to locate his correspondence with the Library of Congress without success. It is assumed that John A. was establishing

credentials for his book since the Mearne letter was included in the publication by Vantage Press which may account for removing his name.

28 *The Journal of Jean Laffite: The Privateer-Patriot's Own Story* (New York: Vantage Press, 1958). [Note: This was copyrighted and published by John A. Laffite [*sic*]. No credit given for translation]; and Mrs. Ray Thompson to Pamela Grunewald, October 15, 1975. Note: Vantage Press of course is the well known vanity publisher and John A. Lafitte paid for the publication.. Incidentally the first editions sold quite well, but most of the stock was lost in the house fire. Copies are quite rare in the market and some have sold as high as $500.

29 *The Spartanburg (SC) Herald,* May 17, 1960, JLC,SHRLRC; and JLCF,SHRLRC. Note: The journal and several of the other documents at the station were singed in the fire, but none were lost. His suit was not very successful.

30 John D. Hyatt, Galveston, to John A. Lafitte, Pacolet, SC, January 2, 1967, letter, JLCF,SHRLRC.

31 Charles Hamilton, New York to John Laffite, San Antonio, July 9, 1969, letter, LSRC, SHRLRC. Note: By 1969 and probably earlier, John A. started occasionally signing his name Laffite rather than Lafitte and when he felt like it, his signature began to mimic Jean's, demonstrating another one of John's peculiarities. When correspondents wrote to John A. Laffite, he never corrected this misspelling of his surname.

32 Don C. Marler, ed. "The Acquisition of the Laffite Journal," *The Laffite Society Chronicles* 4, no. 1 (February 1998): 20.

33 Ibid. 20-22.

34 Ibid, 21.

35 Ibid. Note: Simpson added: "Later, I learned that *Time* had mixed up the pictures. They showed this Mr. Laffite's picture and the article was about another Laffite who was a criminal in New Orleans—a waiter in New Orleans.

36 Death Certificate, South Carolina, JLC,SHRLRC. Note: On the death certificate, his surname is spelled LaFitte.

37 Marler, 21: Ralph O. Queen Report, September 27, 1974, JLCF, SHRLRC.

38 Joyce Calhoon, Liberty, TX, to Judge and Mrs. Price Daniel, Austin, May 8, 1975, letter; John L. Howells, Houston, to Miss Miriam Partlow, Liberty, TX, May 9, 1975, letter; and Joyce Calhoon, Liberty, TX, to Wm. Simpson, Houston, May 16, 1975, letter, JLCF, SHRLRC. Note: The Atascosito Historical Society sponsored from 1973 to 1977 the fund raising for the construction of the Sam Houston Regional Library and Research Center. It also purchased with specified contributions several collections and manuscripts for the center.

39   Receipt of Sale, July 16, 1975, JLFC, SHRLRC.

40   Press Release, Texas State Library and Historical Commission, [now the Texas State Library and Archives Commission] June 9, 1976; and Joyce Calhoon, Liberty, TX, to David B. Gracy, III, Austin, December 10, 1980, letter, JLCF, SHRLRC.

41   JLCF, SHRLRC.

42   Donor Form, Price Daniel to Texas State Library and Archives Commission, August 1, 1978; and Donor Form, Mrs. Price Daniel to Texas State Library and Archives Commission, November 27, 1989, JLCF, SHRLRC.

43   Price Daniel, Austin, to John L. Howells, Houston, June 18, 1975, JLCF, SHRLRC.

44   Lacie Lafitte Sanders was John A.'s widow and ex-wife, JLCF, SHRLRC.

45   Mrs. Ray Thompson to Pamela Grunewald, October 15, 1975, letter, LSRC, SHRLRC. There were two or more bibles in the John's collection which accounts for the discrepancy.

46   Ibid.

47   Some Laffite scholars have disputed this and contend that Arthur may have seen only portions of the collection. In his personal acknowledgments, he states that he relied on former biographies, periodicals, published contemporaneous correspondence, Latours's works, court records, and "as well as correspondence, journals, diaries, Bible entries, and other records belonging to the Laffite family never before published. All placed at my disposal unconditionally and without reservation to their use." He thanked John Adrechyne Laffite [*sic*] of Kansas City, Missouri, for his generosity in sharing the materials. *Jean Laffite, Gentleman Rover,* 286.

48   Many of the questioned originals are not originals, but are entries written by family members in a copy book and on various sized papers. This was fairly common around the turn of the century as a leisure time activity to maintain mementos.

49   Lewis E. Harris, to Mrs. Lula Surratt, June 2, 1955; and David C. Mearne, to John A. Lafitte, September 5, 1956, JLCF, SHRLRC.

50   Frances H. Stadler, "Laffite Documents-Challenge to Validity", *American Archivist* 25, no. 3 (July 1962): 395-396.

51   John H. Jenkins to Charles Hamilton, October 2, 1969, letter, JLCF, SHRLRC.

52   Charles Hamilton to John H. Jenkins, July 28, 1969, letter, JLCF, SHRLRC.

53   Charles Hamilton to John A. Laffite [*sic*], September 23, 1969, letter, JLCF, SHRLRC.

54   Ralph O. Queen Report, September 27, 1974, JLCF, SHRLRC.

55   Ibid.

56   See : Robert C. Vogel and Kathleen F. Taylor, compilers, *Jean Laffite in*

American History, A Bibliographic Guide (Saint Paul: White Pine Press, 1998).

57 Charles Hamilton to Robert C. Vogel, February 26, 1974, letter, LSRC, SHRLRC.

58 Mrs. Ray Thompson to Mrs. Lee Grunewald, October 3, 1975, letter, LSRC, SHRLRC.

59 Ibid. Further examples of letters can be found in the LSRC, SHRLRC. There is not proof that John A. Lafitte made very much money on any of his ventures except for the final sale of the collection. He always seemed to be in need of funds and lived a life style much like any other retiree on a pension.

60 Robert C. Vogel to Pamela Grunewald, October 28, 1975, letter, LSRC, SHRLRC.

61 Robert C. Vogel to Pamela Grunewald, February 13, 1978, letter, LSRC, SHRLRC.

62 Donor Form, Price Daniel to Texas State Library and Archives Commission, August 1, 1978, JLCF. SHRLRC.

63 John Howells to Price Daniel, October 16, 1979, letter, JLCF, SHRLRC.

64 Price Daniel to John Howells, November 8, 1979, letter, JLCF, SHRLRC.

65 Mimi Bethancourt, Resume, 1978, SHRLRC.

66 Mimi Bethancourt to John Howells, November 8, 1979, letter, JLCF, SHRLRC. Note: A strange fact was that Ms. Bethancourt never communicated directly with Price Daniel in terms of the report. It was always done through John Howells even though she was working for Daniel. The delay in transmitting the final report was never explained.

67 Marian Bethancourt Report, letter, JLCF, SHRLRC.

68 Clancy DuBos, "Lafitte: Pirate's Costly Journal May Be Only a Famous Fake", *Sunday Times-Picayune,* June 8, 1980.

69 Charles Hamilton, *Great Forgers and Famous Fakes, The Manuscript Forgers of America and How they Duped the Experts* (New York: Crown Publishers, Inc., 1980), 121, 129. Hamilton developed a tendency to glorify John A. Lafitte referring to him as the "greatest forger in America" especially when he contended that John had forged the Diary of Jose Enrique de la Pena. This forgery certification was published on page 147 in Bill Groneman's book, *Defense of a Legend, Crockett and the de la Pena Diary,* published in 1994. Again, Hamilton was talking off the top of his head since he had never viewed the original diary. He repeated this same charge in 1997 in Dale Walker's book, *Legends and Lies: Great Mysteries of the American West.* Hamilton continued to refer to John A. Lafflin when there is no proof that he used this surname.

70 Ibid., 122-123. Note: in Vogel's defense, it should be noted that he did not appreciate Hamilton's characterization. Vogel was the first person to attempt to understand the provenance of the journal and had collected many letters from people who knew John A. Lafitte.

71 Robert C. Vogel to Price Daniel, June 12, 1980, letter, JLCF, SHRLRC.

72 Ibid.

73 Dr. Regional Wilson Paper, LSRC, SHRLRC; and Pam Keyes, Miami OK, to Robert Schaadt, Liberty, TX, November 11, 1996, letter, JLCF, SHRLRC.

74 Pam Keyes and Dr. Reginald Wilson, "The Saga of the Seal" *Laffite Society Chronicles* 4, no. 2 (August 1998): 2-5.

75 Document: Statement of Robert C. Vogel, 1998, JLCF, SHRLRC.

76 Charles Ramsdell, Jr., "Why Jean Lafitte Became a Pirate", *Southwest Historical Quarterly* 43, no. 4. (April 1940): 465.

Printed in the United States
120456LV00001B/1/A